What *Really* Happened
in Ancient Times

A Collection of Historical Biographies

Compiled by

TERRI JOHNSON

Illustrated by

DARLA DIXON

D1563504

BRAMLEY BOOKS
www.bramleybooks.com

A Division of Knowledge Quest, Inc.
San Antonio, Texas

Published by BRAMLEY BOOKS
A Division of Knowledge Quest, Inc.
4210 Misty Glade
San Antonio, TX 78247
www.knowledgequestmaps.com

Cover Design by Cathi Stevenson
Illustrations by Darla Dixon

Printed in the United States of America
Copyright © Terri Johnson, 2006
All rights reserved
ISBN # 1-932786-21-X

Publisher's Cataloging-in-Publication data

Johnson, Teresa Lynn.
        What really happened in ancient times : a collection of historical biographies
/ compiled by Terri Johnson ; illustrated by Darla Dixon (What really happened…
series, v.1).
        p. cm.
        1-932786-21-X
        Contents: Eve-The very First Days of the World--Noah and the Great
        Flood--Gilgamesh-A Tale of Two Friends--Imhotep-The Man Who Saved
        Civilization--Daniel-Captive in Babylon--Cyrus the Great-Mighty Warrior,
        Gentle King--Eratosthenes-A Friend of Learning--Constantine-By This Sign
        You Shall Conquer.

1. Biography--To 500. 2. Civilizations, Ancient. 3. History, Ancient. 4. Bible--
Biography. 5. Middle East--History--To 622--Biography. 6. Rome--History--Empire, 30
B.C.-476 A.D.--Biography. 7. Greece--History--Biography. I. Dixon, Darla. II. Title. III.
What really happened… series.

CT113 .J64 2006
920.03--dc22   2006908477

Contributing Authors:

Karla Akins
Noah and the Great Flood
Daniel - Captive in Babylon

Jennaya Dunlap
Imhotep - The Man Who Saved Civilization

Kathleen L. Jacobs
Cyrus the Great - Mighty Warrior, Gentle King

Jocelyn James
Constantine - By This Sign, You Shall Conquer

Terri and Nicole Johnson
Eve - The Very First Days of the World

N.R.S. Laurents
Gilgamesh - A Tale of Two Friends

Susannah Rice
Eratosthenes - A Friend of Learning

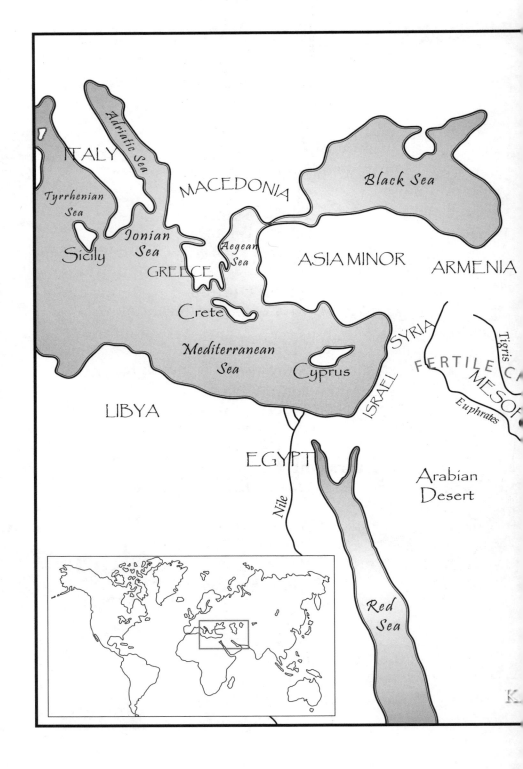

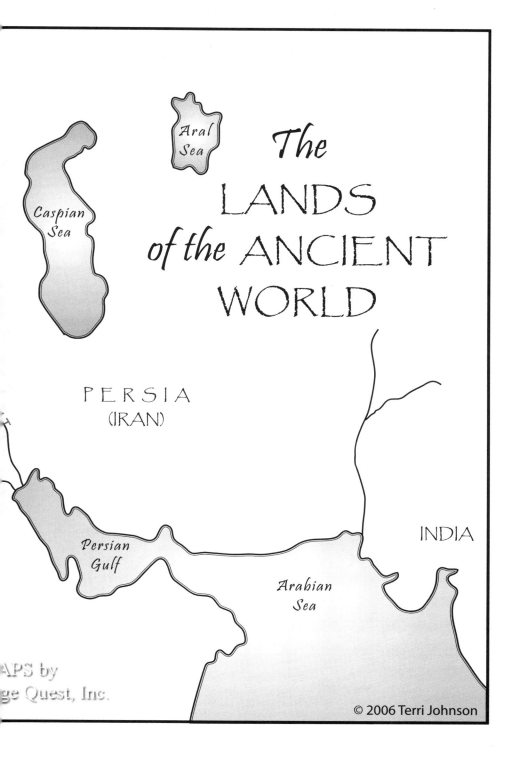

Aral
Sea

Caspian
Sea

The
LANDS
of the ANCIENT
WORLD

PERSIA
(IRAN)

INDIA

Persian
Gulf

Arabian
Sea

Other books in this series:

What *Really* Happened During the Middle Ages
What *Really* Happened in Colonial Times
(scheduled for Spring, 2007)
What *Really* Happened During the Modern Era
(scheduled for Fall, 2007)

e-books also available at
www.bramleybooks.com

TABLE OF CONTENTS

"Brevis a natura nobis vita data est; at memoria bene redditae vitae sempiterna."

"It is a brief period of life that is granted us by nature, but the memory of a well-spent life never dies."

Marcus Tullius Cicero, *Philippic 14.12*

"So teach us to number our days,
That we may gain a heart of wisdom."

Psalm 90:12, NKJV

A Word from the Publisher:

Dear reader, young and old alike,

History is an interesting blend of facts, legends, assumptions and speculations. Historical research uncovers events from the past – how, when and where an incident happened. It cannot, however, fully explain motivations – why someone did what they did – or how an event can be interpreted so differently by two or more eye-witnesses. History is the story of people from the past – people who lived and died based on their convictions and perceptions about the world they lived in. *What Really Happened in Ancient Times* is a compilation of stories based upon actual historical happenings as found in scripture and other historical writings. We, the authors, have been careful not to add to nor subtract from the actual events of history, especially the scriptural accounts. We have, however, added small fictional elements, or daily life details, as to contribute to the flow of the biographies and the ease of reading. In the same way, some unsavory details have been left out or glossed over for the benefit of our younger readers and listeners. We hope that you will enjoy these historical tales of real live people and learn something new about the time period we call the Ancient Times.

Terri Johnson

For Rachel and Lydia, my sweet daughters who love a good story. May you be inspired to do great things - Terri

My part of this story is dedicated to my mother, for giving me the opportunity to help her. Thanks Mom - Nicole

Eve
The Very First Days of the World

*by Terri Johnson
and Nicole Johnson*

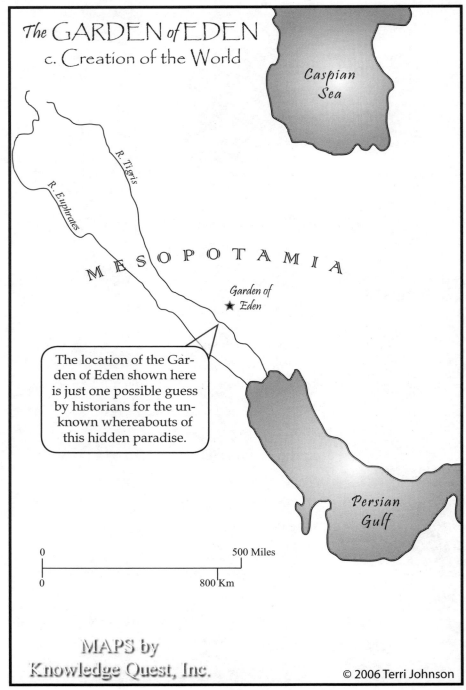

The GARDEN *of* EDEN
c. Creation of the World

Caspian Sea

R. Tigris

R. Euphrates

M E S O P O T A M I A

Garden of
★ Eden

The location of the Garden of Eden shown here is just one possible guess by historians for the unknown whereabouts of this hidden paradise.

Persian Gulf

0   500 Miles

0   800 Km

MAPS by
Knowledge Quest, Inc.

© 2006 Terri Johnson

1
Eve
The Very First Days of the World

by Terri and Nicole Johnson

he long, thick, massive body of the slithering snake began to circle about her, taunting her, enticing her, deceiving her. Its dry scaly coils brushed against her leg, sending shivers up her spine. Once it completed its agonizingly slow circle around her, the huge head of the creature rose up ominously to confront her face to face. The hypnotic ruby eyes of the snake matched the color of the gorgeous apple it held between its jaws. "Eat," the serpent hissed, "Eat and you will become as great as He – powerful, beautiful and everywhere at once!"

Struggling between desire and disgust, she tried to turn away from those eyes, but found that she was riveted in place. Panic rose within her breast and she opened her mouth to scream, but no sound came. She pushed down the urge to flee, mustered her courage and looked the great serpent in the eye with a confidence she did not feel. "Let me go," she pleaded in a faint whisper. "Never," it hissed. The apple it held in its mouth began to ooze and drip from its fangs, like blood spilling to the ground.

The trance broken, the woman turned and ran at an inhuman speed she did not know she possessed. Her feet barely touched the earth as she fled from the temptation that haunted her. Several breathless moments later, she turned to look over her shoulder to find that the serpent was immediately behind her. She tried to run faster, but realized with a sense of dread that she would not be able to outrun this beast.

"No!" She screamed. "No! Not again! Please, not again!"

She awoke from her nightmare in a dripping sweat. With her heart still pounding and her hands visibly shaking, she turned over to the one who would comfort her. She found that she was alone. The pale light of daybreak was filtering into their bed chamber through the reed doorway and she realized that Adam had already risen for the day's work.

In the half light, she scanned the room to see that the children were still asleep. Seth stirred and rolled over, but remained in slumber. The images from her nightmare rushed back to her mind as she considered her children and her hopes and dreams for them. She breathed a prayer to her Maker. *Why, Creator, must I continue to be plagued by these dreams? Is there still a lesson that I have not learned from the garden? God, please, please, erase these disturbing thoughts from my mind and give me peace. Or perhaps you may see fit to tell me the reason for their continual return. Have I not been punished enough? Is your forgiveness not yet complete?*

She lay back on her mattress, pleading silently to the One who brings peace out of chaos. Suddenly a forceful wind blew though the woven reed doorway, rustling the tousled hair upon the young sleeping heads. "Teach your children..." she thought she heard in the voice of the wind. The strange moving air swirled about the room and then past her own head, brushing against her cheek. She heard it again, but this time in the form of a very low whisper meant only for her, "Teach your children..." Her breath came in short gasps as she realized that she had just heard the voice of the One from whom she had not heard audibly in over 100 years. "Teach your children," she repeated to herself. Seth stirred again and stretching, sat up in his bed.

"Mother, did you say something?" he asked groggily.

"No, son, I did not. Or at least I did not mean to," she answered, wiping the sweat from her brow and her disheveled hair from her face. Realizing there would be no more rest for her until the sun began its descent at the far end of the day, she rose quietly and tip-toed out of the animal-skin covered dwelling. Drawing water from the watering hole was the first among many tasks that must be accomplished each morning. Upon her return from the watering hole, she poured some crushed grain along with a portion of the cool water into her stone pot for the morning porridge. She stoked the smoldering coals from last night's fire and then placed the pot directly on them until the mixture was thick and bubbly. She tossed in some fresh herbs for flavor and some dried chunks of fruit for sweetness. Adam loved the way she prepared his porridge at the dawning of each new day.

Two arms grabbed her from behind and she jumped with a start.

"It is only me, dear wife," Adam cooed softly in her ear. "What has made you so jumpy this morning?" Turning into his full embrace, she placed her head upon his broad chest.

"I had the dream again, Adam," she blurted. "I am continually haunted by it." She paused to hear his reply. When none came, she went on. "He spoke to me, Husband."

"Who spoke to you?" Adam inquired cautiously. "The serpent?"

"No, my husband. It was the One," she paused. "It was Creator God from the garden!" She looked imploringly into his eyes.

"Goodness, Wife. Speak! What did our Friend say to you? Did He walk with you as in the days of old in the cool of the garden? Did His presence fill the entire space that you beheld? Did you grow small and weak next to His grandeur and might?"

"Husband, please… one question at a time. No, He did not reveal himself as in the days of the beginning of the world. He spoke to me in a quiet whisper in the form of a strong rushing wind. But I recognized His voice. How could I not? I asked Him why my dream continued to plague me so and He answered by saying, 'Teach your children!' And that is all. He spoke no more."

Adam dropped his arms from around her and walked away several paces. He turned and walked back. "I, too, heard His voice, but it was in the form of a dream. I didn't recall it until now," his voice trailed off.

"What did He tell you, Adam?" He opened his mouth to speak when Seth and his younger sisters emerged from the doorway of their home.

"It was just one word," he quietly answered her. "He said, 'Remember'."

Without a word, the children went about their morning routine. Seth removed the heavy pot from the fire pit and began to stoke the dying embers, adding more brushwood and timber to fuel the flames. The girls filled gourd bowls with the delicious porridge and brought the steaming food to their parents where they still stood, staring at one another as though in a trance.

"Father, Mother, the meal is cooked and ready for you. Will you not come around the warmth of the fire and break your fast?"

"What? Oh. Forgive us children, we were… that is, our thoughts were elsewhere," Eve said as she sat down on the skins which were arranged neatly beside the fire pit for the morning meal.

Sensing some unspoken tension, the children were quiet as they ate their porridge.

Eve stared into the dancing fire. Her mind kept drifting back to her dream and the Voice that she had heard in the wind. What could He have possibly meant by "teach your children"?

17

I thought I was teaching them! Eve mused silently to herself. *Every day I teach them skills as we go about our endless tasks. And what was Adam supposed to remember? Have we forgotten something?*

"Mother?" Seth's words broke into her reverie.

"Yes, my son?"

"I am off to tend the sheep, if you no longer need me here."

"No, I do not need you. Go along with your father," Eve said, rising to her feet. She embraced her tall and lean 11-year-old son, planting a kiss on his forehead. Adam gave her a long and reassuring look that promised they would talk more at a later time. She turned and picked up the cooking pot and beckoned to each of her daughters. The girls shook out the skins from around the fire and carefully folded each one. They collected the gourd bowls and utensils and followed their mother down to the watering hole.

Once the dishes were washed, dried and put away, the girls tidied their indoor and outdoor living quarters while Eve swept the packed dirt floors. Next, the goats were milked and then Mother and daughters fetched their woven reed baskets to gather produce from the orchard and garden on the far side of the brook. They picked juicy sun-ripened figs and glossy pink pomegranates. Clusters of powdery grapes were beginning to purple on neatly trimmed vines. In the garden, the girls dug up an assortment of root vegetables, careful to save their delicate green tops which would make a wonderful addition to their evening meal.

Throughout the course of the day, Eve contemplated God's words to her. *Teach your children,* He had said. *Remember,* was His command. All the while she was working alongside her daughters, she thought about His curious and important message delivered to her and Adam. Sometimes she would catch herself looking off into the distance absently. She had to force herself to concentrate on her work, and still her thoughts drifted from her tasks and her normally pleasant conversation with her girls.

At the end of the day, after supper, the family once again encircled the roaring fire. One of her daughters spoke up. "Mother, you have been distracted today. Is there something wrong?"

Eve brought her hot herbal drink to her lips, inhaling the soothing aromas of mint and lemon as she considered how best to answer this question.

"Yes, children, I... I have been distracted, as you say." She paused again, then decided to speak plainly. "Early this morning before I arose, the Voice of God came to me in the wind."

"What did He say?" the children exclaimed, their voices a mixture of excitement and anxiety at the same time.

"Well," Eve replied, "He said simply *'teach your children'.*"

"Did He mean us, Mother?"

"Yes, I believe so, dear ones." Eve said slowly.

"Did He say more?" queried Seth, "As in *what* you are supposed to teach us?"

"No, Seth, He just said *'teach your children'.*"

All eyes turned to Adam as he began to speak his churning thoughts. "I have been dwelling on this all day long,

19

just as you have, Eve. I believe that He means for us to teach you children about Him, and His wonders, and perhaps even about our own mistakes and failures."

"Yes, Adam, now that you say it, I know that you are right. This is what the Lord wants from us: to teach our children about Him!" Eve responded with excitement. "When shall we begin?"

"I should think," said Adam reverently, "that when you hear His Voice, which has been silent for over a hundred years, you had better do His bidding quickly.

Taking her usual place beside Adam, Eve asked the children if they would like to hear a story.

"Oh, yes, Mother!" they cried. They pressed closer, so they would hear every word of the tale she was about to tell.

"Yes, but what shall we tell them about first?" Eve said, who was eager to do God's bidding, but was unsure where to start.

"Well, starting at the very beginning seems wise, does it not, Wife?"

"Yes, Husband, but if we are to start at the beginning, then you had better go first. Because children, Adam was created before I was. You see, we were not born into the world like each of you. In fact, we were never tiny babies or even half-grown children. The truth of it is that Adam lived several days before the Creator fashioned me. So, go ahead, Adam, tell them how it all started."

Adam cleared his throat and said, "Alright then, we will tell you of the garden and the very first days of the world. Children, draw close to me and feel my skin, touch my hair, look into my eyes. Would you believe the Creator God formed me out of the very dust of the ground? Your mother had an even more startling beginning." Adam winked at Eve. "Now, can you imagine the incredible power it takes to create a living, breathing creature from the dirt? We cannot imagine such might! But that is how powerful and mighty our God is." The children pressed their toes into the soft dirt at their feet as they contemplated their father's words.

"After six days of bringing our world into existence[1], he chose to create a likeness of Himself. And I am he. The Master Creator who spoke a single word and the earth appeared, also made me." Adam thumped his chest with both hands. "I am humbled when I think of it because He is so great and majestic. He says that I bear His likeness. Simply amazing!" he said, shaking his head.

"Father," Seth interrupted, "What does Creator look like? Does He look like you?"

"That, my son, is a most challenging question! No, He does not look like me. I am but a dim reflection of Him. He has features, such as we do, but He is everything that we are not. His eyes are like fire, piercing and yet warm and inviting. His mouth issues words that ring with strength and authority. The earth trembles when He speaks." Adam paused as he considered how else to describe His Friend from the garden.

Eve spoke, "His legs are like towers of might; his arms are like wings, downy soft within His embrace."

---

[1] To read the full story of how God created the earth and everything in it, read Genesis 1-2 in the Bible.

21

"You know, Eve," Adam continued. "There were times in the garden when I marveled why our Friend had created the sun. Yes, I knew it was a magnificent sphere giving us light. But we already had light, for He was our light, and the sun... well, it is only a dim reflection of Him. And the trees... were they not gorgeous, Eve? And yet, there were times also that I marveled that He had created them for He was our sustenance. He was our shelter. His arms provided our shade and rest. Of course, now I understand."

"Tell us when you met Mother," chimed in one of the children.

"Ah, your mother...What a delight she was to my eyes that very first day and she still is even now. I had been given the task of naming all of the animals, for God had given me dominion over them. I observed and commented to my Lord that I was different from the rest. Each of the animals had mates for companionship and to help populate the earth. I did not have such a mate.

"Upon hearing my words of dissatisfaction, Creator God immediately struck me down and I passed into a deep sleep. When I awoke, I felt a throbbing pain in my chest that at first I attributed to my unexpected fall. But then I saw her standing before me. She was the most beautiful creature I had ever seen. I found out later that she was fashioned out of one of my ribs, which, of course, explained the pain in my chest!"

Eve continued, "As soon as The Creator breathed life into me, I stood up, and there on the ground before me was your father, looking dazed. He was the first thing I ever saw in the Garden of Eden. Those were glorious days, were they not,

Adam? We were young and in love, carefree and in harmony with our Maker. Such days will never be again."

"Why not, Mother?"

"Because of my disobedience, son. I ate of the forbidden fruit when I was explicitly told not to. I talked your father into eating as well."

"Yes, dear, but you were deceived by that hideously beautiful serpent. Even so, I was, and still am, responsible for my own actions and disobedience. I could have made a different choice, but I, too, was lured by the serpent's crafty deception.[2] I wanted the same thing that you wanted – power, glory and omnipresence. I wanted to be as great as the One who had created me! Oh, it is such a lie that the created could ever be as great and marvelous as the Creator. And yet I believed the serpent, just as you did, Eve."

"Children, hear us well. This is when everything instantly changed. Before our Lord even appeared to us that evening in the cool of the garden, we knew we had done something terribly wrong. Our shame hung heavily upon us and we hid from Him behind the lush foliage. We were mortified! We had gone directly against the command of our gracious Friend. He told us that we could eat from any tree, except for one – He called it the tree of the knowledge of good and evil. And yet that was the very tree that we did not resist.

"Before we even saw Him that evening, we heard Him calling our names. 'Adam! Eve!' The voice, in which

---

[2] To read the rest of the story about the serpent's deception and the fall of mankind, read Genesis 3 in the Bible.

we once took boundless delight, now sent shivers of panic through our bodies! Our fear was well-founded, for that day we were cursed. After a pathetic attempt to dodge our own responsibility and cast the blame on others, we were driven from the Garden of Eden by the Lord's mighty angel, never to return. We were indeed cursed that day. We lost not only our home, our sustenance, and our peaceful way of life, but our daily intimate fellowship with our Maker as well. I was sent to toil in the fields and your mother was cursed with pain in childbirth."

"What happened to the serpent?" asked one of the girls. "It seems to me that he was perhaps the worst of all and certainly deserves some kind of punishment."

"Ah, the serpent," said Eve. "Yes, he too was cursed. He must forever slither along the ground on his belly, despised by the greater part of God's creatures, most prominently me. And the other half of the curse I did not understand. Something about him bruising the heel of my seed and my seed crushing his head.[3] I did not comprehend this then, nor do I now. I do know that 'my seed' refers to our offspring, but I do not see how our children have yet or will in time 'crush this serpent's head'.

---

[3] "The Seed of the woman is the Promised One, the coming Messiah of Israel. Bruise His heel speaks of a serious injury, but it is contrasted with the crushing of his head – the defeat – of the serpent, or Satan. When Jesus went to the cross, He was bruised in His heel. That is, he suffered a terrible but temporary injury (John 12:31; Col 2:15). In His resurrection, He defeated His enemy. From that moment on, Satan has lived on borrowed time. He is already defeated; only the announcement of victory needs to be made (see Rom 16:20)." From the Nelson Study Bible, copyright 1997 by Thomas Nelson, Inc. Used by permission.

Some things in life remain a mystery, I suppose."

"Life outside the garden was barren and dry," she continued. "Our first days were miserable and we thought we would perish. We were hungry, dehydrated and bitterly cold when the sun went down at the end of the day. Our first task was to find a reliable water source and set up shelter. Then, without delay, your father set to work and, after much toil, raised a handful of crops for harvest, and gathered a good number of animals to shepherd and butcher for food. As time wore on, my belly began to expand and I felt movement inside. Lo and behold, I was with child! Upon his astonishing and painful birth, we named him Cain. He was the joy of my life. Some years later, Abel was born. His birth was just as astonishing and certainly just as painful! Yet, he was the delight of my soul. Were those not amazing years, Adam? Those rambunctious boys kept us hopping, so full of energy, so full of creativity. We could never sit still as they were always getting into trouble![4] Ah, I loved them with all my heart!"

Eve dropped her head into her hands and began to sob. How could a mother describe the loss, the pain, the heartache? How could she describe the deep ache that squeezes her heart whenever she reflects on her short time with her beloved boys? *Oh Father,* she breathed desperately, *Only You can heal my grieving heart!*

"But Cain still lives, Mother. Does this not bring you any comfort?" Seth asked tenderly, intuitively feeling his mother's agony.

---

[4] To read the exciting tale of Cain and Able, turn to Genesis 4 in your Bible.

"Cain walks in sin and defiance against the Lord. He does not recognize his Creator, nor the parents who raised him. It is as though we have two dead sons." Adam placed his arm about his wife's trembling shoulders and continued, "Children, we made some grievous mistakes with our two older boys. We did not teach them diligently about the Lord, our Maker and our Friend. Now I see that this is what He wants us to do differently with you. He wants us to teach you about Him so that you can lead a long and purposeful life in the land[5], so that you can tell your children and your grandchildren after them. Listen to our stories as we tell them to you tonight and again tomorrow and the night after that, for we still have much to tell. We have painful stories to share with you as well as ones that will bring much laughter and joy. Remember them and tell them to your children and to your children's children. Bind these stories of our Lord on your hearts and minds, so that sin and disobedience do not overtake you."

Silence descended upon the small family as they huddled together about the dying embers of the fire. The darker the night became around them, the more brilliantly the stars shone overhead. No one wanted to speak and yet no one wanted to leave. Eve looked from her husband of many years to her young children who had full lives yet ahead of them. Her mother's heart longed for a way to keep them always safe – from temptation, from sin, from the angry hand of another.

---

[5] To read about Seth's "long and purposeful life in the land", read Genesis 4: 25-5:8 in your Bible.

Yet she knew that she could only do the bidding of her Lord. At this moment, she realized with an inexplicable assurance, all was well. She would rest and take comfort in this thought tonight. As if by an unspoken cue, their three children stood and crept quietly into the tent. Adam and Eve followed behind.

The End

About the Authors:

Terri Johnson is the creator of Knowledge Quest maps and timelines (www.knowledgequestmaps.com). Her mission for the company is to help make the teaching and learning of history and geography enjoyable for both teacher and students. She has created and published over 20 map  and timeline products. Her *Blackline Maps of World History* have been widely recommended in the education community and published in *The Story of the World* history series by Susan Wise Bauer. Terri and Knowledge Quest recently won the "Excellence in Education" award granted by The Old Schoolhouse magazine for best geography company of 2003 and 2004. Terri resides in San Antonio, Texas with her husband Todd and their five children whom she teaches at home.

Nicole Johnson is Terri's eldest daughter. She has three younger sisters and one brother who keep her entertained most of the time. Nicole, who is 12 years old, has homeschooled since kindergarten. She has many hobbies and pasttimes, when she is not doing her schoolwork. She enjoys reading, writing, sewing, making candles, swimming and spending time with friends. She loves the rain and the beauty of nature. Nicole stays in touch with her long distance friends through the convenience of modern email and blogging.

To my precious son: Noah Emmanuel. May you, like Noah of old, walk with God, hear His voice, and obey His commands no matter the cost.   Never forget your unique purpose or doubt your mission.   I love you!

Noah
And the Great Flood

by Karla Akins

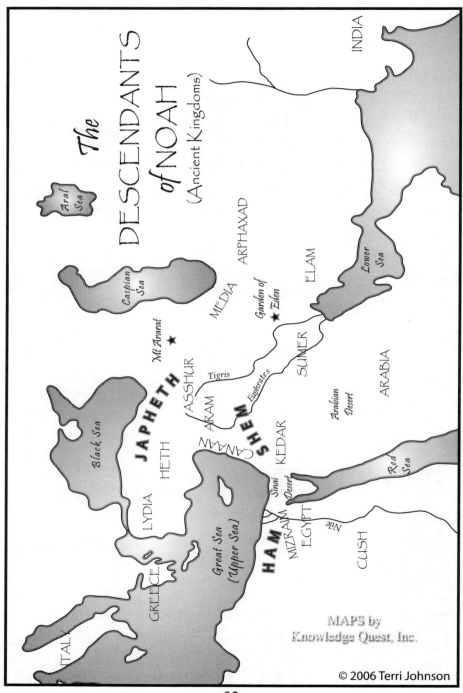

The
DESCENDANTS
of NOAH
(Ancient Kingdoms)

Aral Sea

Caspian Sea

INDIA

ARPHAXAD

MEDIA

Garden of
★ Eden

ELAM

Lower Sea

Mt Ararat ★

ASSHUR

Tigris

Euphrates

SUMER

ARABIA

JAPHETH

ARAM

SHEM

Arabian Desert

HETH

CANAAN

KEDAR

Black Sea

Red Sea

LYDIA

Sinai Desert

Nile

GREECE

Great Sea
(Upper Sea)

MIZRAIM

EGYPT

CUSH

HAM

ITALY

MAPS by
Knowledge Quest, Inc.

© 2006 Terri Johnson

Noah
And the Great Flood

(This story is an educated guess of what it might have been like for Noah
and his family, based on Genesis Chapters 6-9)

by Karla Akins

oah's wife hummed a song as she finished
chopping the last of the radishes. She
placed them in a copper bowl with the other
vegetables and tossed them with her slender
brown hands. This was her husband's favorite
dish, and today she wanted it to be perfect. The delicious aroma
of garlic breads baking in the circular hearth filled the air. A
flat smooth stone in the bottom of a pit made a perfect oven for
all of her main dishes, pastries and breads. Her daughters-in-
law worked beside her, slicing vegetables and grinding grain.
Besides the different squashes, there were other delicious fruits,
vegetables, nuts and grains piled high in baskets and bowls all
around the cooking area. Colorful cabbages, ripe black olives,
crunchy spinach, garlic, leeks and various kinds of aromatic

spices surrounded the women, their delicious smells making them hungry.

Noah's wife picked up a small clay pot of olive oil and sprinkled it over her pile of chopped vegetables before tossing them. She smiled thinking of how Noah would enjoy the evening's meal. She was planning a private dinner tonight with just the two of them.

They had been too busy lately with all of Noah's successful business ventures. It had been a long time since they had dinner alone without all their sons and their wives. Something had been troubling Noah the past few days, and she hoped that tonight he would tell her about it.

She set out plenty of small clay lamps and made sure they were full of olive oil. The sun would be going down soon, and she didn't want to be looking for oil in the dark. Shem's wife had been collecting thin cotton gauze bags brimming with fireflies. They were a soft source of light for a dinner for two, even better than candlelight. She hung a dozen or so of the firefly bags in the tent and placed them around the beautiful crimson blanket she had spread on the ground for their meal.

Noah's wife had embroidered the edges of the blanket with sparkling rocks, jewels and beads. She enjoyed pretty things, and now she placed two fluffy matching lounge pillows, trimmed with gold beads and thick luxurious tassels, at one end of the blanket. She placed silver trays full of fruits and nuts and a steaming bowl of rice and raisins in the middle between two miniature clay lamps. There were apples, figs, grapes, dates, and melons – all of Noah's favorites. She liked making the mealtime pretty and attractive, even though Noah teased her about it.

"Ham!" she called to her youngest son, who was tending sheep – or so she thought. She saw him peek up at her from over the next hill. She sighed realizing he must be looking for baby dinosaurs again. He had loved studying them since he was a little boy.

"Yes, Mother?" Ham replied, placing a tiny dinosaur in the pack he was wearing over his shoulder.

"Where is Japheth?" his mother asked. "I asked him to help with the cattle this evening."

"He is with them. And before you ask, Shem is with Father in the city."

"Have you secured the sheep and the eggs for tomorrow?"

"Yes, Mother," he said, grinning at her with sparkling deep brown eyes. She looked at him admiringly. He had grown strong, tall, kind and good. His brown skin shone in the sun and his curly brown hair framed his pleasantly bronzed face.

"Begin to bathe for dinner, Ham. You and your brothers will be dining alone with your wives tonight so that I may dine alone with your father."

"But Mother, when you and Father aren't with us my brothers tease us about being newly married and sing and play the same embarrassing songs over and over again."

She shook her head. "No, Ham. Besides, you do your fair share of teasing and singing." She pointed to the bag wiggling at his side.

Ham grinned and hugged his mother. She tousled his

hair the same way she did when he was a small boy.

"Okay, Mother. I still need to secure the sheep, then I can get ready for dinner."

After the vegetables were chopped, she called to her daughters-in-law to begin plating the molokhia[2] and beans while she bathed and dressed to meet her husband at the end of a hard day.

Noah was over 500 years old, and she was not much younger, but she still enjoyed getting dressed up for him and surprising him with new garments. He would often bring her sparkling jewels and gold and silver bracelets from his trades with the merchant sailors on the shores of the Black Sea. Even though Noah did not approve of the lifestyles of the people he met, he was very successful because he was honest and operated with integrity. Most merchants couldn't be trusted.

She chose her favorite frock: a flowing purple tunic with tiny gold threads running throughout it. The bodice was encrusted with tiny jewels Noah had brought her from his excursions in the countryside. She loved wearing this one because it made Noah light up to see her in it. She chose a gossamer, violet-colored scarf to go with it and headed down to her favorite bathing spot in the pond behind their home.

Walking home from his day of trading, Noah could see the lamps glowing in front of his tent and smiled. He knew that his wife would be requesting his company privately this evening. After living together for hundreds of years, they could almost read each other's minds. But the past few days,

---

[2] A nutritious soup made from molokhiyya, a type of greens.

he knew, she was not able to tell what had been troubling him. Somehow she sensed his need to talk to her, and he was grateful. He could always count on her to understand, and it comforted him.

"Shem," he said to his son walking beside him. "Your mother and I will dine alone tonight. Please tell your brothers."

"Yes, Father," Shem said, hugging his father. "Good evening and give Mother my love."

The father and son each went their own way. There were squeals and loud giggles coming from the large tent where his sons, their wives and servants would dine. He was thankful for a peaceful, solitary dinner.

"Good evening, husband," Noah's wife said, kissing him tenderly on the forehead. "You look tired." She caressed his silver locks and patted his shoulder tenderly. She smelled wonderful, Noah thought, and he admired how beautiful she looked in her purple gown. It was his favorite.

Noah hugged his wife tenderly. "I am indeed very tired tonight," he said, with the weariness of hundreds of years in his voice. "You smell like roses, and the meal looks delicious, Wife." He had tried to put energy in his voice, but it didn't work.

"All your favorites," she said. "My best tunic, my special salad and your favorite bread."

"Wonderful," he said smiling. "Let me go down to the reeds and bathe, and then I'll join you."

Noah's wife handed him fresh, clean garments and kissed him again on the cheek.

"I'll go get the bread," she said. "By the time you're

finished, I will have everything ready."

Noah went to take his bath while she removed the mouth-watering breads she had made for the evening meal from her oven in the ground. They were browned to perfection. Noah would be so pleased.

Back at Noah's tent, she set the bread and a jar of honey-butter on the colorful blanket to the side of Noah's plate. After she scooted everything around on the blanket exactly to her liking, she set to work lighting more of her lamps.

Finally her husband returned, refreshed from his bath and hungry.

"I'm famished," he said. "Let's pray and give thanks, Wife, and then let's eat!"

She bowed her head and prayed with him, holding his hand and whispering prayers of thanks. In the distance they could hear people shouting, children crying, and women screaming. They knew that once again their neighbors in the city had drunk too much wine and were having parties, ignoring their responsibilities, and neglecting their families and children.

"And Lord," Noah prayed. "Please help me to warn them. They don't hear me. But give me the strength not to give up. Amen."

Noah's wife looked into his eyes and saw concern and pain in them.

"Noah," she murmured, as she kneeled and filled his dish with salad, "warn them about what?" She tore off a piece of bread for him to eat and handed it to him. "What is it? What has been troubling you so?"

"God has spoken to me, Wife."

"So what has He told you?" She asked, taking his hands and pulling him down to the blanket beside her.

Noah didn't answer. His wife looked into his eyes again, and saw grave concern.

"My dear husband, tell me, what is it that puts such deep wrinkles in your forehead and concern in your eyes? What could be so worrisome that the Lord cannot solve it?"

"We will need to be very strong, Wife," he said. "Stronger than we have ever been before."

She nodded and placed her hands on his. "Of course, husband, you know I will do whatever God wants us to do. Now tell me. What is it that has my husband ignoring his favorite meal this night?"

"God has told me..." He paused, and looked into his wife's beautiful imploring eyes. "He has told me that he has seen the wickedness of man and that every imagination and thoughts in his heart are evil continually."

She nodded. That was true. She could hear their raucous music and violent screams even here in the safety of their own rural garden.

"Go on," she said. "What else did He say?

"He said that He was even sorry that He had created mankind, and that it grieved Him."

Tears streamed down Noah's face and his wife stifled a gasp. She busied herself with the food, arranging and rearranging it, and worked hard to keep her voice steady.

"Are you sure you understood Him?" she whispered, not daring to look again at her husband.

"I am sure. I am sure because He also told me that He is going to destroy every person and beast and creeping thing and birds. He is sorry He made them."

Noah's wife cried out and dropped a tray of fruit, her hands flying to her chest as if to stop the pounding of her heart.

"Oh, Noah, surely it was only a bad dream. Surely…"

"It was not a dream, Wife. I know the voice of my God when He speaks."

"But our family! Our friends! What will become of us?" she cried, looking into his eyes now, searching for answers.

"Dear Wife," he said, taking her gently into his arms. "We can be thankful that I have found grace in the eyes of the Lord." She trembled and he hugged her gently, trying to calm her.

"Oh, Noah, I am so thankful you are a man who loves the One True God. It is what I love most about you."

Noah kissed her softly on the forehead and looked into her eyes.

"He has given us a job to do. It will take many years and much faith. I will need your support and the help of our sons."

"Of course, my husband," she said. "Anything that God says to do, I will do. I trust Him with my life."

"It is good that you do, Wife, for He has entrusted us with an enormous responsibility."

She poured him a cold glass of goat's milk and tried not to let him see her hands shaking.

"So, tell me," she said. "Don't keep me in suspense."

"I am to build a boat."

His wife laughed nervously. "A boat? Is that all? As if you've never built a boat before! That is not such a hard thing."

"Not just any boat, Wife, but a giant ark of safety. No one has ever seen such a ship. God is going to send a flood to destroy everything. And the only thing that will save our lives is to be on that boat."

"A flood? What is a flood?"

"God is going to cover the earth with water."

"How?"

"It is going to rain."

"Rain?" she asked. "What is rain?"

"It is when water falls from the sky."

She couldn't imagine such a thing. Water had never fallen from the sky before. Every morning mist rose up from the ground and watered her vegetable and flower gardens, her orchards, and all the earth perfectly.[3]

"Water as deep as the sea will cover the entire earth and every animal and person not on the ark. Nothing will survive that is not on the ark with us – except for some of the fish of the sea."

His wife began to weep. Noah took her into his arms to comfort her.

"Wife," Noah whispered. "Hasn't God protected and cared for you for hundreds of years? And haven't I led you into safety time and time again?"

She nodded. It was true. There was violence all around her family, but Noah, with the help of God, had always managed to protect his family from the impurity of the world

---

[3] Some scholars believe a gentle rain may have fallen on the earth during this time, but in Genesis 2:5-6, mist rose up from the earth to water it.

around them. He had provided well for them by working hard, and God's blessings were abundant as he obeyed Him. But his family had been obedient, too, and Noah knew that was just as important as his leadership.

"Why would His mercy change now?" Noah said. "God has promised to help us. But it is not going to be an easy task. We have to do our part."

His wife sniffed and nodded and turned to the trays of fruit. She placed a plump fig on Noah's plate along with some olives. She had no idea of the future, but she knew that with the help of Noah and the Lord she would endure it.

"Ham should begin to work with me at a shipyard we will prepare on the plateau in the midst of the nearby forest," Noah said. "I will not need to build the ark by the sea because the sea will come to us, and I will need an abundance of timber and pitch."

"I am sure the children will be agreeable to that," his wife said.

Noah sighed. "I will need all the boys to help me, as well as hire help, and we will need to put oxen and mammoths to use helping us move lumber."

"That will mean we will need to cook extra each day," she said. She was already planning menus for an army of workers.

"It is a good thing you like animals, dear lady."

"Why do you say that?"

"Because, we are to build a boat big enough to rescue them all."

She dropped the basket of dates in her hands, spilling them onto the lamps and splattering oil all over the beautiful blanket. The flame flickered and went out.

"*All* the animals?"

Noah gave a loud and hearty laugh, his eyes sparkling with mischief. The look on his wife's face was exactly as he pictured it would be when he told her. He knew that her mind was spinning at the thought of such a task.

"Well, every *kind* of animal at least," Noah chortled.

"Do you have any idea how big a boat that will take?"

"I do."

"Noah, are you sure? I mean, are you sure you didn't just have a bad case of indigestion after eating your daughter-in-law's beans?"

Noah threw back his head and laughed again. The noise in their sons' tent went silent, as they listened to their father's hearty laugh.

"No, dear wife, I am quite sure it was God's voice and not beans."

"How on earth will you ever build a boat big enough? Where would you even start?"

"God has given me specific instructions. He told me exactly how big to make it."

"And who will ride on this boat?"

"We are all to ride in it. Us, our sons and their wives, all the animals and anyone else who will heed the Word of the Lord and join us."

His wife sat in stunned silence, staring off into space. She was trying to imagine being in the midst of so many animals in one place. How would they live? What would they eat? How would they clean up? What about the smell? How would she possibly keep the place clean?

"Noah, are you sure we can't have our own boat?"

"I have to obey the Lord. He has spoken, and I will obey."

"But it sounds so impossible!"

"It's not, Wife. You know that nothing is impossible with God!"

Reluctantly, she nodded.

"Listen," Noah said, finally eating the delicious food his wife had prepared. "Think about it – most of the animal types are small – only a few are large."

"But what about the Brachiosaurus?"

"We will take the younger ones – they aren't so big."

"But I thought you said all of them?"

"Not all of them, Wife, just pairs of each kind. Well, at least of the unclean ones. Of the clean ones we are to take seven."

"There aren't as many clean ones, so that's a good thing I guess," she said.

Noah nodded. "I have given it a lot of thought. The average size of most of them is the size of a cat. And most animals live in the sea, so they don't need to be on the boat. We are only commanded to take those who breathe through their nostrils."[4] He bit into a fig and grinned at his wife who looked at him in awe.

"Noah, Noah, Noah," she sighed. "You are always full of surprises."

~~~~~~~

---

[4] Genesis 7:22

Over a hundred years later, Noah stood inside the ark, inspecting the work his sons, workers and he had completed.

"It is exactly right," Noah said. "Good job, sons."

"Thank-you, Father," Ham said. His voice was barely audible above the crowd outside. They were throwing old pots and rotten vegetables at the great ship, yelling names and taunting Noah and his family.

"How long do you think they will stay today?" Shem asked.

Noah shook his head. "I have no idea. But they will get the same sermon today they've gotten the last 100 years: repent and be saved."

"I admire your unshakable faith, Father," Japheth said. "Were it not for your love for God and our family, I am afraid I would think you were as crazy as everyone says you are."

Noah laughed and patted his son on the back. "Well, I'm not denying that I'm peculiar. I just know what God has commanded me. And I must obey."

His sons nodded their heads and went back to work putting the final touches on the ark. Noah went outside, dodging the things the crowd threw at him. He climbed on top of a high beam and began to preach

"Listen people of the earth!" he shouted. "God has told me that the earth has become corrupt because it is filled with violence!"

"Oh, Noah!" someone yelled. "Where ya goin' in that big box of yours?"

"Not very far!" someone else yelled. "There's nothing to

steer it and just look at how flat it is!"

The crowd laughed. Some drank wine and danced, making fools of themselves. It made Noah so sad. He had been preaching for over a hundred years now, and yet no one would listen.

"God is going to bring a flood of waters upon the earth to destroy all flesh and everything that is in the earth will die!" Noah shouted. "This ark is an ark of safety! Those who repent and turn to God will not die if they come aboard!"

"Rain, rain, rain, rain!" the people chanted, over and over again, laughing and mocking Noah. His entire family had been ostracized since he began building the huge ark. People who were once their friends had left them. They were scorned and belittled. No one wanted to be friends with the crazy man and his family who built a giant boat on land.

Still, Noah's family obeyed him and believed in what God had told him, even when it didn't make any sense. They had to admit that the dimensions of the boat they were building were amazingly perfect and able to hold a multitude of animals. Even Noah's wife had come to realize that the ark was perfectly suited for the animals and her family. The way the windows at the top brought in fresh air and let out the stale air was thrilling to her. God had even thought of her, she thought, when He designed the stalls to slope ever so slightly to make cleaning after the animals easier.[5]

"Just perfect," she thought. "Just like He is."

News of "that crazy man Noah" and his sons building an over-sized ship had traveled far. For a hundred years people had traveled for miles just to see it. They had watched and laughed as it grew longer and longer. In fact, it was 450 feet long![6] No one had ever seen a ship that big, and they thought Noah had lost his mind.

"He's going crazy!"

"His poor wife; married to a lunatic!"

"Hey, Shem, Ham and Japheth! Your dad is a fool!"

"Who builds a ship on a hill in the middle of a forest?"

The people were more cruel and rude in the beginning of construction than they were now that the ark was nearly completed. They had lost interest in that "crazy man and his family in the country" and had gone about their daily routines – making plans for the future, marrying, reveling, and worshipping nature and other make-believe gods. They continued to build magnificent cities and increase their technologies. They were more interested in what they themselves were building.   They lived for entertainment, feeling good, and having lots of material possessions. They were just too busy to listen to a gray-haired man preach from up high on his giant boat.

One day, Noah and his family were inside the ark, hanging lamps and putting final touches on the family's living area when they heard a cacophony of sounds coming from outside.

"Oh, no, the crowds must be coming again – I hope there's not another riot," Noah's wife said. She was putting jars of honey on a shelf that Noah had fashioned with a bar across the middle to keep them from falling.

---

[5] This is a fictional speculation.
[6] 300 cubits.

"The last time they completely ruined my roses. I just got them blooming again – I hope they stay on the other side of them."

"Mother, Father, look!" Ham shouted. He was standing at the door pointing at something on the next hill.

In the distance there was a large dark object approaching. But as they watched and looked closer, the object broke up into hundreds of smaller ones. As the objects came nearer they could see it was a gigantic herd of animals - walking and vocalizing - and heading straight for the ark!

"God must have told them to come," Ham's wife whispered.

"Oh no!" Noah's wife cried. "My roses!" Two young wooly mammoths and seven young bison were trampling through her flower garden.

"My darling wife," Noah said. "They will soon all be under water anyway."

"But I worked so hard. . ." She sighed, threw up her hands, and turned to filling water jugs.

Suddenly, seven baby giraffes ran up the wooden ramp and entered the ark.

"Catch them!" Noah said.

"Yes, Father!" his sons shouted, chasing after the lanky youngsters and securing them. Soon, everyone was busy gathering up animals and placing them in their proper places. Noah's wife had to stop filling water jars to help manage the animals. They were all surprisingly gentle and cooperative, but as soon as they had one group settled, another came.

"They're eating all the melons!" Shem's wife cried.

"We harvested plenty of melons," Shem said. "Relax and look at how much they enjoy them!"

Noah and his sons were fascinated with all the creatures standing outside the ark munching on the surrounding foliage. Pairs of birds in every color, shape and size were flying around and perching all over inside and outside of the ark. There were seven birds each of chickens, ducks, songbirds, pheasants and countless other clean kinds. The animal noises were deafening and the family had to shout to hear one another. But Noah could still hear God's voice, and he was able to know exactly how to make the animals comfortable.

He also knew what would make his wife and daughters-in-law feel at home, and had constructed a cozy living area in the middle of the ark.[7] Each of his sons and their wives had their own little rooms for privacy, and they all shared the kitchen area in the middle of the ark. Noah's wife was delighted with the sunshine that poured in from the windows at the top of the ark. She was actually looking forward to preparing the first meal in her new "kitchen."

It took them just seven days to get the animals and Noah's family all settled and ready for their adventure. In between loading animals, food, and supplies, Noah preached to the onlookers outside. People were beginning to gather and watch as the "crazy family in the country" loaded all the animals that came to them. Even animals they had never seen before emerged from their hiding places to board the ark.

---

[7] The Bible doesn't say where the living quarters for the family were in the ark or what they were like.

Because so many trees had been used to build the ark, some animals had no more hiding places nearby. During the last few years, animals had spent their days watching Noah curiously as he worked on the ark and checked measurements according to God's design. He had collected a menagerie of animals as they had come to him, and he never tired of studying them.

Noah's family worked until they were exhausted, but there was more to do. Animal bedding had to be thick and placed on all the decks of the ark. It was at least three-stories high! Noah was relieved when he discovered how roomy God had designed the ark.

The aviary was Noah's wife's favorite. Even though the birds' calls were deafening, she loved seeing them all perched in a row and she lost count of the many different colors. She wanted to memorize them and use them in new frocks.

She had cleverly fashioned drinking vessels and feeders for all the animals. She made sure the aviary and each stall had a pot full of water standing upside down in a clay dish as well as a clay grain hopper of a similar design. These trickled water and food to the animals in perfect timing and gave everyone a more flexible schedule in which to replenish all the creatures' food and water supplies. [8]

The animals snuggled right in to their homes peacefully without a struggle. Ham brought on a colorful little dinosaur the size of a kitten and another one just like it. He was busy

---

[8] A theory of how the animals could have been easily cared for on the ark.

caring for all the reptiles on the top deck where the sun could reach them from the lookout windows above and was enjoying their complacency. Usually they were far too fast for him to catch! Had God somehow spoken to the animals and asked them to cooperate? Ham wouldn't be surprised. That was the kind of God he loved and worshipped. He thought of everything.

Shem and Japheth were busy with the cattle and other mammals. Their wives and mother were busy stocking the pantry for the human passengers, and making sure there was plenty of bedding. Noah's wife shed a tear thinking of the homes they were leaving behind forever. But then she quickly brushed the tears away as she caressed some of the lovely blankets she had made and spread them gently over Noah's resting place.

Aromatic flowering vines had grown into the ark and had covered the beams and railings in the last 100 years. The fragrance of the flowers and fruit vines would help mask the smells of all the animals. Now that Noah's wife was in the ark and experiencing its simple beauty, she was thankful for her husband's keen mind and ability to understand the directions God had given him. It was, in fact, a perfect place for animals and humans to dwell in harmony.

Three levels of stalls and cages lined the outer walls of the ark, and the animals seemed to be right at home. Alpacas, wooly rhinos, and even great wild cats were all calmly at rest in their stalls.

Japheth walked into the ark's "kitchen" with two baby chimps – one on each hip.

"Look, mother!" he said. "Aren't they adorable?"

"They are very sweet," his mother said. "They look just like you, Japheth." "Mother!" Shem's wife said, "You joked!"

"I did," she agreed. It had been a long time since she had smiled. She had been so worried about the ark, the animals, and her family. She had been so sad about her friends who refused to believe in the One True God. There had been so much work to do from sunup to sundown and it had been a long time since she had felt like smiling. But now, seeing the ark completed and all the magnificent animals peacefully settling into their new homes – it gave her a renewed faith that God really was in control and really would take care of her family during the flood.

"Is everyone in?" Noah shouted, racing into the room. "Where is everyone?"

"We're here father," Noah's family said, gathering around him.

"God will shut the door soon," he said, sadly. But, he was also relieved his family was safe on board.

His family looked at one another with mixed emotions. They could hear the crowd outside, yelling, shaking the torches they carried, banging drums and mocking Noah and his family.

Why can't they just believe? Japheth thought. *Surely they can see the hand of God is with this ark. Surely they can see even the animals obey him.*

I will miss my friends, Shem thought. *If only they would believe and be saved.*

Noah's daughters-in-law were weeping. Some of their relatives were outside, but no matter how much they had begged – they would not join them on the ark.

"Noah, there is still so much room left on the ark," his wife said.

"God knew what He was doing," Noah said. "We could take more than 45,000 sheep-sized creatures with us and still have a lot of room left for more people and provisions."

"Yes," she said. "I see that now. We have so much room to spare. If only people would believe and be saved, Noah." She had tears in her eyes, and Noah cradled her in his arms. His sons were comforting their wives and encouraging them to focus on the beautiful animals.

Suddenly -- the door -- began to move!

"God is shutting the door." Noah whispered. "He is shutting the door Himself. This way those outside will know it is not I, but God that has done this."

As the door began to shut, the shouting outside changed to questions. *How was Noah able to shut such an enormous door? He had no winch – where were the ropes?* Still, no one yet believed that Noah would be traveling in water in his boat.

Inside the ark there was a sudden peace, as if the animals knew that something momentous was about to take place.

Then, the earth began to shake violently! The people outside the ark began to run and scream – why was the earth moving? Up from the earth sprang great fountains of water. Volcanoes erupted and rain and lava fell from the sky. Rain fell in torrents. The people outside the ark had never seen rain – or felt it fall on their skin – they were terrified!

Some of them began to panic and banged on the ark – "Let us in! Let us in! We believe now! We believe!" But it was too late. The door was closed, and Noah could not open it.

Japheth's wife, overcome with anguish began to run up the ramps to the windows on the top floor.

"No, my daughter!" Noah cried. "Do not go – it is not for your eyes to see."

Japheth pulled his wife from the ramp and held and rocked her. Everyone's face was wet with tears. The sounds from outside the ark were heartbreaking.

"Why!?" Shem's wife cried. "Why could they not believe? Couldn't they see how God brought even the animals to safety? What made them think they would be safer than the fowls of the air and the beasts of the field? Why wouldn't they listen!?"

No one slept that night. Instead, they sat up in the kitchen, listening to the deafening sound of the wind and rain. They had never heard such sounds before – it sounded like thousands of little hammers banging on the roof and sides of the ark. Noah's family simply sat that first night, holding one another and praying.

Days later after falling asleep at the kitchen table, wrapped in one another's arms, they were all awakened by a sudden lurch! Ham and his wife fell off the kitchen bench to the floor, and Noah held tightly to his wife. They were moving! The great ark had slipped from its dry dock, and as the timbers beneath it slipped away it began to gently bob in the water. Because of the way God had designed the ark, there was very little yaw, and no one got seasick.

For forty nights the rain fell. The women wrapped their scarves tighter around their heads and held their hands over their ears as the thunder clapped and the wind screamed and

roared. Some nights it was hard to sleep, and they got their days and nights mixed up because the sky was dark with clouds and pouring rain. Noah's wife mourned the loss of sunlight from her windows. With the help of her sons, she lit the lamps in her kitchen. The animals, sensing danger, slept.

The Ark bobbed in the water – never tipping over, never crashing. It floated perfectly in the raging water just as God had designed it.   Finally, on the 41st day, Noah's wife awoke to see something she had sorely missed: Sunshine streaming in from the windows above!

"Noah! Noah!" she cried. "Wake up! It's not raining!"

Everyone woke and ran to the ramps leading to the top of the ark. When they looked out they all gasped. The sunlight was blinding, and as far as they could see there was water – nothing but miles and miles of blue-green water. Their homes, their friends, their other relatives, had all vanished beneath a great sea.

"My sons," Noah's wife said with tears in her voice. "Look at your father – he is the father of the world now. Because he listened and obeyed, we are safe. He did not give up for one hundred years when he could have easily been discouraged. Because of his faith, his descendents, your children, will repopulate the earth."

Noah's lips quivered and tears streamed down his face. How could he begin to fathom the great mercy of God? His mind could not contain it.

"How long, Father, before the water recedes?" Shem asked.

"I don't know, my son. We will wait on the Lord."

For 110 days the water kept rising with mighty power, covering the highest mountains on the earth. Then, a terrible wind came, causing the waters to abate. After about 74 more days of bobbing up and down on the waters there came a great "thud!"

"Land!" Ham cried. They all ran again to the narrow top floor lookout to peer out the windows. As far as they could see there was a vast ocean of rolling water surrounding them.

"We have landed on a mountain," Noah said. "There is still too much water to leave the ark."

After living in the ark on the mountains of Ararat for 40 more days, Noah finally sent out a raven and a dove. The raven did not come back, but Noah knew that ravens were scavengers, and would eat things clean animals would not. The dove returned to the ark because it couldn't find a livable place to land. After another seven days the dove was sent out again. This time, it returned with a fresh new olive branch.

"I have something for you," Noah said, handing his wife the olive branch.

"Where did you get this?" she asked, amazement in her voice.

"The dove brought it back to me."

"Does that mean...?"

"That means in about a week, my dear wife, we will be leaving this fine ark and setting the animals free."

Noah's wife was elderly, but that didn't stop her from squealing with delight and throwing her arms around her husband's neck and giving him a big kiss on the cheek.

A week later Noah let the dove go again, and this time

it did not return. Noah knew that very soon, God would be instructing him to leave the ark.

Finally, the day came. Noah and his sons hewed out an opening in the side of the ark and they all stepped out into a brand new world. The animals were close behind, leaping and running, flying and singing their own praises to their Maker. They had been on the ark for 371 days, and it was magnificent to run free!

The air seemed different somehow. Noah could see that things were not the same as they were when they had gotten into the ark. But they were alive, and they would all make a new start.

"Come," Noah said. "We are going to build an altar and offer a sacrifice to God."

Together they built an altar, made a sacrifice, and thanked God for His great mercy and goodness to them.

"Look!" Noah's wife pointed to the sky. "Noah, Look!"

Noah and his sons and their wives looked up into the sky and saw a beautiful rainbow. Before they could ask what it meant, God blessed Noah and his sons and said,

"…This is the token of the covenant which I make between me and you and every living creature that is with you, for perpetual generations: I do set my bow in the cloud, and it shall be for a token of a covenant between me and the earth. And it shall come to pass, when I bring a cloud over the earth, that the bow shall be seen in the cloud: And I will remember my covenant, which is between me and you and every living creature of all flesh; and the waters shall no more become a flood to destroy all flesh."[9]

~~

Thousands of years later in 1400 A.D. at a campfire in the middle of the forests of what would become Minnesota, a wise old Ojibwe native sits at a campfire telling his grandchildren the story of a time long ago when harmonious life ceased and men and women disrespected each other, and families quarreled.

"The villages began to argue back and forth," he said. "This saddened the Creator greatly. He decided he must purify the earth through the use of water. The water came and flooded the earth. All but a few of each living thing survived. But one man survived by floating on a log in the water with all kinds of animals."

Today, there are over 500 flood legends that have survived and developed in nearly every region on earth. They are about a man in ancient history who built a boat and saved the animals and his family. The legends are overwhelmingly consistent, and people around the world, when they see a rainbow in the clouds, still remember that God keeps His promises.

See *About the Author* on page 163.

---

[9] Genesis 9:12-15, KJV

To all who believe that without knowing our history, we will not have much of a future.

Gilgamesh
A Tale of Two Friends

by N.R.S. Laurents

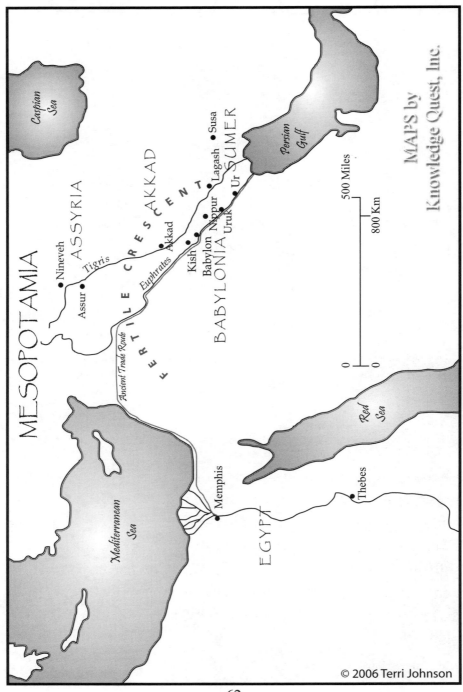

MAPS by
Knowledge Quest, Inc.

© 2006 Terri Johnson

3

Gilgamesh
A Tale of Two Friends

by N.R.S. Laurents

The sun was beating down hot and bright. The broad river flowed lazily in the summer's heat, lapping the muddy shore, touching the hulls of the many barges and boats lying on the banks. The tall mud-brick ramparts of Uruk rose imposingly into the deep-blue sky just to the north, sheltering huts, houses, palace and temples alike from the sun's rays. An afternoon breeze rustled the reeds along the river. It rose off the shallows, flapping the sails of the fishing boats and the bright shifts of the sailors, ran through the shady orchards of apple and pomegranate trees, passed over the towering outer walls and swept across the city, stirring the fronds of the acacia and palm trees.

On the roof garden of the royal palace, Gilgamesh the

king stretched sleepily as the breeze ruffled his dark hair where he lay amid cushions by the side of a shallow pool. Its waters stirred, glittering under the sun, the deep blue of the sky nearly as dark as the glazed azure tiles lining the shallow basin.

There was none greater in Uruk than Gilgamesh. Born the son of King Lugulbanda, his mother was the goddess Ninsun, who was unsurpassed in beauty and loveliness by any mortal woman in the lands through which the rivers Euphrates and Tigris flowed. In manhood, he was tall, strong as a wild bull, and as handsome as a god. The people of Uruk liked to boast that this was because Gilgamesh was, after all, only one-third a man and two-thirds a god.

His accomplishments, regal stature and good looks notwithstanding, Gilgamesh also had his share of pride and arrogance, often using his royal power in ways the people disliked. He exulted in proving his physical prowess in combat with anyone under a staid middle age. Since he invariably won all such contests, the townspeople had many of their sons either to mourn or to take to the temple healers. Gilgamesh also had a keen eye for beauty, and cheerfully pursued all the prettiest women of Uruk, whether married or not.

So, as much as he was admired and regarded with pride by his subjects for his kingly might and magnificence, many grumbled about his high-handed ways, and earnestly prayed to their gods to curb the king's destructive whims. It is said that the gods took heed and made another man very like Gilgamesh in order to direct him toward more acceptable pursuits. That man was called Enkidu, and he lived in the wild.

While Gilgamesh relaxed in Uruk, Enkidu was running on the grassy plains with the deer and the antelope. He, too, was strong, fleet of foot, not quite as tall as Gilgamesh, but dark and handsome, with long black hair flowing down his back. He was a wild man and lived among the wild animals of the grasslands. He drank at their waterholes and helped them by filling in the pits dug by trappers. Together they ran free across the fertile plains of the broad river valley, slept out under the stars, and roamed far from the cities of Sumer to the feet of the forested mountains of the north and east. Over time, a trapper in the area wearied of losing his prey and finally took a beautiful woman named Shamtar to meet Enkidu, to entice him away from the wild animals.

Shamtar was a priestess of Ishtar, the goddess of love, and Enkidu was as impressed with her beauty as she was with his splendid good looks. He left the wild, and they went to live among the shepherds of the plains, where Enkidu protected their herds from lions and learned the ways of civilized men. It was there he heard tales of Gilgamesh, king of Uruk, of his grandeur, his prowess in combat, his strength in battle. While Enkidu had lost some of his strength and swiftness since leaving the wild, he was still as strong as a savage bull and the shepherds admired him greatly. Hearing about the famous king of Uruk, Enkidu grew curious and decided to visit the great city to challenge Gilgamesh to a trial of strength.

Late one afternoon, as the hot breeze died down over the marshes and the city came alive with music and dancing, Enkidu approached Uruk's southeastern gate. For miles he had followed the river road through small farms and large estates, their fields of wheat and barley stretching far across the plain. The trade road from Ur passed through Uruk to Kish and was much traveled by foot-sore commoners, proud herdsmen leading their flocks, and merchants stringing along camels laden with the riches of Sumer. In the distance, where the river broadened into a silver band, barges showed like dark smudges against its shining surface, and smaller reed-boats dipped their oars as they moved along the horizon.

Enkidu marveled at the many new and splendid sights, but nothing had prepared him for his first glimpse of the city, surrounded by fields and orchards, spread between the road and the river. Uruk's walls and gate-towers, fashioned from millions of sun-dried bricks made from the mud of the life-giving river, rose majestically into the darkening sky. Just visible above the wall were the temples on their proud ziggurats, with the tops of many slender date palms lending a touch of color. As he neared the gate, Enkidu joined a stream of travelers hurrying to enter the city before the gates closed at full dark

He moved with the crowd along the broad street leading into the center of Uruk, where the large temples and the royal palace were located. The street was lined with one- and two-story mud-brick houses where artisans, merchants and scribes lived. To right and left, narrow roads and winding lanes led into busy bazaars and bustling markets. Down one, Enkidu could see fruit-sellers' wares displayed under large woven tarps strung between the houses to provide shade for customers and merchandise alike. Down another he saw the meat market, along with sellers of grains and cereals. Further on he saw a street crowded with women eager to select the best the wool-vendors had to offer, to turn into finely spun yarns and the hand-loomed cloth for which Uruk was famous. Cloth from Sumer could be traded as far north as Kanesh in Anatolia for jewels or gold.

Finally, Enkidu reached the foot of the temple of Anu and Ishtar and stopped to stare in awe at the gigantic structure before him. The temple, as was the custom, was built on a tall ziggurat, to raise it high above the recurring flood-waters. Many terraces and steps led up to the temple, which was decorated with colorful tiles and imported wooden columns. The wild man had never seen so grand or so glorious a building. It seemed even to rival for height the forested slopes of the far mountains where Enlil, father of the gods, had set Humbaba the giant to watch the trees.

Around the bottom of the ziggurat sprawled a large number of huts and houses, a whole city within a city. Craftsmen, servants, priests, and slaves lived and worked at the foot of the temple mount, to serve the gods, to earn their goodwill for the people of the town.

Turning aside, Enkidu saw his goal in sight. The royal palace was only slightly less impressive than the temple, its gate decorated with large stone tablets depicting heroic deeds by past kings in finely carved relief. The huge double doors stood open and two armed soldiers idly watched the open square. Enkidu strolled across purposefully.

"I am a stranger to Uruk," he hailed one of the guards. "Is this where Gilgamesh, king of Uruk, has his abode?"

The soldier had turned his head to watch his approach, his eyes round with wonder at the unusual height and exotic bearing of the stranger. Not only was Enkidu taller than average, deeply tanned below his dark locks, and broadly muscled, but over his plain tunic he wore a gorgeous lion-skin stretched across his shoulders. The soldier goggled at the man who wore it so casually.

"Indeed, sir, this is the king's palace," he answered. "If you have come to have speech with him, you must hurry: The king is about to leave for the house of Amrahel the councilor, to attend his daughter's wedding."

This was unwelcome news to Enkidu. For a moment he stood in thought, debating whether to postpone his errand until the next day.

"The house of Amrahel is only a short way down the street," the guard said, interrupting his reverie.

Enkidu's eyes flashed. "I will await the king there," he decided. "Where do I find this house?"

After listening closely to the guard's explanation, he nodded with satisfaction. "My thanks for your aid."

He turned away from the palace gate and headed back across the square to reach the tree-lined street the man had indicated. It better suited his purpose to challenge the king on his way to a private celebration than to accost him in his own palace, in front of his servants and ministers, on his throne perhaps, gorgeously appareled and bedecked with jewels and all the insignia of his high rank. Tonight, he might hope to find the king walking alone, or at least with few to witness their encounter, and in clothing more suited to a fight.

In keeping with his resolve, Enkidu did not enter the house of Amrahel the councilor once he reached it. Instead, he positioned himself across the narrow street in a dark doorway and observed the stream of festively dressed visitors. However, no one immediately came who fit the description the shepherds had given him.

His time spent running with the wild antelope of the plains had taught Enkidu patience, and he was inured to waiting. No lion stalked his prey with more quiet determination than he that night, awaiting the coming of the king. Enkidu expected to meet the king with little delay. His composure, however, remained unshaken two hours later when the noisy celebration and the busy town alike began to settle down for the night.

Finally a late wanderer turned up the street. Enkidu straightened eagerly at the sight of the tall, proud figure. When a stray beam of light showed a glint of gold on the man's brow and on his shoulders, he stepped out of his shadowy corner into the road.

Gilgamesh strode along with careless grace, eager for a look at the youthful bride. He invariably arrived only after the ceremonies of the given occasion were over, as much because lengthy rituals bored him, as out of a certain unconscious arrogance. He did not like crowds, and preferred to make himself scarce.

As he neared the house, he became aware of a man directly in his path, barring his progress in a quietly determined fashion that Gilgamesh had never experienced in all his days as crown prince or king. His respectful subjects assiduously made way for him and his servants whenever he appeared in public, bowing to him from a deferential distance.

Nonplussed, Gilgamesh halted a few paces from the stranger. From the light of the newly risen moon and the illuminated windows up and down the street, he viewed with amazement the wild figure clad in a lion's skin, the tanned face under the mane of black hair falling down upon shoulders as broad and powerful as his own. His hesitation lasted only a moment.

"Make way for the king," he demanded calmly, deeming the stranger's singular behavior more a matter of ignorance than of intentional insolence. "Behold, I am Gilgamesh, son of Lugulbanda, king of mighty Uruk. Out of my path, lest you suffer my displeasure for obstructing me."

Almost he moved on, taking instant obedience as much for granted as breathing. However, the stranger did not stir. Instead he spoke, and though his appearance was rough, his voice was pleasant enough.

"Mighty king, I have traveled far to meet you," Enkidu began. "Tales of Gilgamesh and his great strength and wondrous deeds have spread to the remote corners of Sumer and beyond." There was no subservience in his voice or humility in his stance. Instead, there was more than a hint of curiosity as he continued.

"I have heard much of you since I came to live among men, and it would fain seem all was true, for the like of you I have never seen, save when I have beheld my own image in the mirror-surface of a still pond on a calm day."

Being unused to the open scrutiny he met in the stranger's dark eyes, Gilgamesh raised his brows at his daring as much as at his odd tale. He could not suppress a smile as he returned the other's probing glance in equal measure.

"There does seem to exist a certain likeness of shape and coloring between us," he admitted after a closer look. "But tell me, are you man or god? And what is the purpose for which you have sought me?"

It was Enkidu's turn to smile, his face taut and eager: "Man am I, like you, O king, and made of the plain dust of the earth. I have come to Uruk to fight you, and test your strength against mine." And, dropping the heavy lion-skin to the ground a safe distance behind him, he stood at the ready.

The king's eyes lit with a fierce fire.

"Have you indeed?" he demanded. "Grant me time to strip off my royal accoutrements and a fight you shall have, and welcome."

When his opponent merely nodded, he proceeded to take off the thin ribbon of gold which kept his shoulder-length hair off his brow, the broad necklet of gold, lapis and stone-beads which he wore across his shoulders, and the two heavy, jewel-studded bangles off his sinewy fore-arms. Tucking his long tunic into his belt he crouched, balanced on the balls of his feet, his arms coming up as he asked:

"Ready?"

Enkidu lunged.

What followed brought half the population of the street out upon them and wrecked the fronts of no less than three of the nearest houses. Locked in a tight embrace, the two men swayed back and forth, their feet pounding the dusty ground as they moved first to the right, then across the street to the left where Gilgamesh backed into a wooden doorpost with enough force to shake the porch it supported. Another onslaught of the heaving bodies pushed the post off its foundation altogether, and some brick dust sifted down on the fighters' backs as the sturdy cedar post thudded into the road.

Hooking one foot around Enkidu's right ankle, Gilgamesh pulled the leg out from under him, and both fell together as the challenger lost his balance. The king was uppermost to start with, but soon fortunes were reversed as Enkidu got one strong arm around the other's throat. Nearly out of air, Gilgamesh was beginning to see dark spots swimming before his eyes when the wild man forced him undermost and sat on his chest with all his considerable weight.

A nearly super-human effort dislodged Enkidu just long enough for the king to lunge to his feet, and soon Gilgamesh was trying his best to throttle his opponent. Muscles bulged, bones creaked, the dust rose about their feet in veritable clouds, while people from the neighboring houses kept a safe distance, awed as much at the forces unleashed by the struggle, as dismayed at the destruction wrought by the two combatants.

Another porch got smashed as Enkidu managed to break the king's grip on his windpipe. Then for a while both men grappled with each other, bashing into the surrounding walls, plaster and fragments of dried mud liberally raining down upon their shoulders. Neither seemed able to get an advantage over the other, equally matched as they were. Both were determined to win the fight.

Suddenly, Gilgamesh bent his knee, took Enkidu around the waist, and heaved with all his might. Surprised, the wild man did not immediately defend himself as the king lifted him bodily off the ground. With a tremendous effort Gilgamesh threw Enkidu from him, several paces across the street, only to hasten after him and kneel on his chest.

The fall had knocked the breath so thoroughly out of him that at first Enkidu could do nothing but gasp for air, choking on the dry dust. When he found himself pinned by the king's great weight and looked up into the fierce, eager face above him, suddenly Enkidu laughed as he relaxed.

"I make my submission. You have won!" he declared, still chuckling. "But next time take care--you have taught me a new trick this day, which I will know well how to evade when we meet again."

Gilgamesh rose, freeing him, but looked on puzzled as the wild man got to his feet.

"Why do you laugh? It was a fair fight."

Enkidu nodded, but could not help smiling. "Indeed it was. I did not mean to imply aught else. Just look at us, though: Your own men could not tell us apart after this dust-bath of ours!"

Gilgamesh followed his counsel and found himself smiling in turn: They resembled tall clay statues, covered from head to foot in thick reddish dust that hid the color of their hair, the weave of their raiment, the tone of their skin. Almost identical in build and height, even their stature could not give away their identity; only the length of their hair allowed any distinction between them, for even the features of their faces lay

74

disguised under layers of dust, tracked by runnels of sweat, and coated in pieces of plaster that had stuck to them as they rolled on the ground.

At last Gilgamesh glanced at the towns-people watching them from a safe and suspicious distance and he too laughed.

"You are right; they do not know what to make of us. We could be sons of the same mother, you and I, so alike are we in everything, even our strength. It was a glorious fight! I have never come this close to being bested, and if we fight again, the end of it might easily be different, for we are evenly matched. Come, let us not remain rivals! We were surely destined by the gods to be brothers."

He embraced the wild man and they laughed again together as some of the plaster fell off their clothes at the touch.

"I've not had a friend before," Enkidu admitted. "It will be something new for both of us."

Gilgamesh nodded: "There never was anyone to hold his own against me before. We must test your skill with weapons. Just think of the great deeds two men like us could accomplish together!"

Enkidu noticed that the thought seemed to please the king greatly, and smiled again.

"Perhaps we had better fix this mess and get cleaned up first," he suggested, a twinkle in his dark eyes.

Gilgamesh raised one dusty brow as he looked around at the settling clouds of dirt, the shattered porches, and the fallen plaster.

"I suppose we ought to," he said, and there was a note of surprise in his voice, as though he had just discovered the

damage they had caused. "I shall give orders immediately."
He waved peremptorily to one of the more respectable of the
onlookers.

"You there, I shall hold you responsible for seeing to
it that these houses are repaired properly. When the work
is done, send to the palace and present your bill to the royal
treasurer."

The man bowed in acknowledgement of the royal
command, and Gilgamesh put one hand on Enkidu's shoulder.

"Now, let us be off to the palace for a bath, for I confess I
certainly need it. You will accompany me, won't you?"

Enkidu had been a silent onlooker as the king so
summarily dealt with the business at hand. Now he cocked his
head to one side to look up at Gilgamesh, his gaze thoughtful.

"That depends, O king. I do not mean to spurn the
hospitality you so generously offer, but I fain would know what
position you would have me assume in your household. I am
used to being my own master, not any man's servant."

Gilgamesh blushed under the thick covering of dust and
sweat that hid his features. "I thought we agreed to be friends
and brothers," he protested. "No servant of mine shall you
be, and my household and subjects shall treat you as though
you were another son born to my own mother. If you found
my invitation lacking in civility, I crave your pardon: I am
more used to giving orders than speaking to men who are my
equals."

The twinkle back in his eyes, Enkidu reached up to lay
his right on the king's hand.

"Your invitation was courteous enough, and if you yet

lack anything in the consideration of others, I will endeavor to teach it you, as a good friend should," he said. "I have always found it sound procedure to treat all honest men as my equals, and as such, entitled to my respect in equal measure, be they commoner or king."

There was a wave of appreciative murmuring among the bystanders, but the wild man continued, as though he had not noticed:

"In the meantime, a bath would be very welcome, so we had better collect our things and be off or the sun will find us still talking when it comes to look down upon Uruk in the morning."

Gilgamesh bent down to pick up the royal insignia which he had so unceremoniously shed at the start of their fight, then said, as Enkidu did likewise with his belongings, "Perhaps afterwards, while we eat, you will tell me the story that lies behind that magnificent lion-skin of yours, for I love nothing better myself than a hazardous hunt, unless it be a glorious fight at arms."

Seeing the light in his eyes, Enkidu smiled again, and of his own accord embraced the king this time.

"Gilgamesh, you shall hear the story, and we will have many wonderful bouts against each other. Truly there is not another like you among men, and it is no wonder with your great strength and skill that you were chosen by the gods to be king."

"For my part," he continued, "I shall be eager to hear the stories you have to tell of the world, for I know you have traveled much, and I have never been farther from the plains that raised me than this city of yours. Thus we shall teach each other many new things, and have great adventures together, if that is your desire and the will of the gods. Men will tell yet more tales of your exploits to their children, and their children's children, until the end of time. Such are the rewards of a truly noble friendship."

The king nodded. "That is a fair bargain and a glorious future to contemplate, though in all honesty, I doubt anyone will remember me for more than a few generations." He chuckled unexpectedly: "Then again, perhaps the two of us together will raise enough dust for the tales of our fame to make a more lasting impression. Come, we shall talk more of this!"

So saying, they walked off down the street, hand in hand.

In the weeks that followed, Gilgamesh set his heart on undertaking an excursion to the distant mountains, where large cedar forests grew, to cut down the mighty cedars said to be guarded by the giant Humbaba. No trees with wood of comparable quality grew near Uruk, and to build great edifices and adorn the temples, hardwood trees were a necessity.

The members of the council of Uruk warned that to take the cedars belonging to the gods would cause trouble. Enkidu warned that to incur the displeasure of the gods would surely bring misfortune upon Gilgamesh and any who went with him. But the king did not heed their advice. Instead, he ordered made a set of splendid new weapons, worthy of a daring undertaking and spectacular deeds of valor.

Gilgamesh knew he needed the blessing of the gods for the quest to prosper, so he went to ask Ninsun, his mother, to petition their favor. She willingly did so, but also came up with another way to ensure his safety. She officially adopted Enkidu as a son and charged him to go with Gilgamesh on his perilous journey and to do everything in his power to bring him safely home. Enkidu assented. If he could not talk Gilgamesh out of the dangerous venture, he would brave the ire of the gods and the might of the giant guardian of the trees to fight at the side of his friend and brother.

Ecstatic, Gilgamesh promptly had another set of weapons made for Enkidu to match his own. Each received a magnificent axe, bejeweled sword, and bow.

The two adventurers were far from Uruk and nearing the mountains by the time it occurred to Gilgamesh that his companion was in a less than boisterous mood. Relaxing in front of the shelter they had built for the night, at the small cook-fire lit to heat up their evening meal, Gilgamesh watched as Enkidu sat silent, his powerful arms clasped around his knees, his dark eyes fixed unwaveringly on the flames.

"Tell me the thoughts in your heart, my friend," Gilgamesh said finally, resting his chin on his arms.

Enkidu looked up with a hint of a smile. "You know them already," he suggested. "From the first, I told you that this enterprise to cut cedars will likely bring the wrath of the gods upon us, if Humbaba doesn't kill us first."

Gilgamesh nodded. "You have told me so, and the elders of Uruk have said much the same. Yet my mother asked the favor of Shamash to be upon us, and though your heart isn't in this venture, I know it is not because you are a coward. So we will fight the giant together, and together we will conquer. The tale of our travels will be sung throughout the cities of Sumer and our names will be great in the hearing of men."

Enkidu looked at him, the gaze of his dark eyes steady.

"Have you ever seen the giant?"

Gilgamesh shrugged. "No, I have never gone this way before," he admitted. "Yet, how daunting can he be? Why, they call anyone a giant who is taller than most men!"

Enkidu laughed, but without real mirth.

"If you think rumor has exaggerated his size or his prowess, my brother, don't be deceived. I have seen Humbaba from afar when I was running with the animals of the plains. He is a full head taller than either one of us, and his arms are each the thickness of a sturdy cedar. What's more, the gods shield him with their might."

"That may be so, or not," Gilgamesh commented with a shrug. "In any case there are two of us against his one, and we are not inexperienced in the arts of combat. Or has your heart grown faint within you?"

"Not at all," Enkidu replied with a sigh. "The matter bodes ill with me. But if you are determined to do this, I must go with you. Our hearts must be fearless lest we risk all. So let us take what sleep we may, and go on tomorrow to meet the giant. We are near the edge of the forest already, and it is said that he knows immediately when someone enters it, though he be far away."

"Old wives' tales, most likely," Gilgamesh scoffed, as he pulled the fags apart to put out the fire. "I am glad you are not turning back, though. Vanquishing the giant would be little pleasure to me without you by my side, my friend."

Enkidu nodded, stretching himself out in his blankets within their shelter. "So be it, then. Sleep well, my brother."

When at length they reached the forest, Gilgamesh marveled at the girth and the height of the trees. The sheer loftiness and density of the forest giants allowed no ray of sunlight to penetrate to the forest floor except in rare clearings. As he wandered about, eagerly inspecting the trees, Enkidu stood listening for any sign of the guardian giant's approach. What he heard instead was the thud and whack of a great axe nearby, and whirled to see Gilgamesh energetically attacking the trunk of a stately cedar.

In the distance an angry shout went up, followed by a far-away roll of thunder.

"The giant comes" Enkidu shouted over the noisy axe-strokes to warn Gilgamesh. The king nodded but did not stop his efforts, and the cedar was felled before they saw aught of its appointed guardian.

When Humbaba appeared there was little time for them to worry about his exact height, or the best strategy for their attack. He was huge, he was angry, and he was upon them in a flash.

Gilgamesh stood rooted to the ground, axe in hand, while Enkidu drew his knife. As the giant turned towards the king, Enkidu realized that panic must have seized his friend at the awful sight of Humbaba. Enkidu could not fault Gilgamesh for his reaction. The giant was clothed in filthy rags, his face and skin streaked with dirt and dried blood, his hair tangled

81

with roots and vines of the forest. His bulging eyes glared at them with hatred, and his crooked teeth were pointed and sharp, like the teeth of a wild beast about to tear its prey.

With a shout, Enkidu leaped to the ready in case of need. Luckily Gilgamesh heard his brother's voice, and with a cry, jumped back out of the giant's path, his momentary paralysis overcome. His axe flashed, and his first downward stroke bit deep into the giant's neck as the monster rushed by. With a tremendous roar of rage and pain, the giant turned.

A harsh gust of wind swept through the clearing, and a sudden rush of swirling dust blinded the giant, allowing Gilgamesh to strike a second time. Thunder rolled close by, clouds rushed across the mighty tree-tops as they bent before the wind. A third blow finished the creature off. His heavy body fell to the ground, his hideous face hidden from view, as a steady rain began to fall on the forest.

Enkidu stepped to his brother's side and gazed upon the dead thing that had been their fearsome foe. "You have slain him as you intended," he said. "The cedars of his forest are yours for the taking. But spare the far Cedar Mountains where the goddess Ishtar abides. Enlil will be angry enough as it is."

Panting from exertion, Gilgamesh shook himself as the rain began to run into his eyes. "I will. If I had realized how awful he was and how huge, perhaps I would have lent more of an ear to your warning. Why, he is just like a tree himself, only a lot more dirty."

At that, Enkidu could not help but laugh. "Oh, my brother, you have slain the giant with your axe, you have done the impossible and felled him like that cedar you took first. You almost got yourself killed going up against him, and here you stand, marveling at the unwashed and filthy rags of him."

A sudden rueful grin lit the king's face at his words. "I suppose that is rather unimportant, considering what we've been through," he admitted. "I have never come this close to death. But for your shouts, I would surely have perished at the giant's hands. I owe my life to you, my friend."

They clasped hands, standing in the warm summer rain, the giant's dead body at their feet. Then Enkidu, ever practical, gave a sigh.

"I don't suppose that in addition to the axes, the royal weapon-smiths packed us any shovels?"

Gilgamesh looked puzzled. "No, why do you ask?"

"Unless we mean to leave this carcass to the wild beasts of the forest, we shall have to dig a sizable pit to bury it," Enkidu pointed out. "I can think of few tasks less pleasant."

The king looked around. "There are rocks in abundance here. Let us collect them, and cover his body with branches and stones instead."

Enkidu's face lit up with the first genuinely pleased smile since they had left Uruk. "I hasten to obey, O mighty king!" he joked, as Gilgamesh bent down to wipe the blade of his heavy axe in the grass. "And when you are done cleaning your weapon, you may as well start cutting the branches we'll need."

Thus did Gilgamesh and Enkidu vanquish the mighty Humbaba and return victorious and unharmed to Uruk, on a raft of cedar-trees they cut with their great axes in the giant's forest.

The tale of their adventure grew more unrecognizable

with each retelling, until Enkidu saw fit to warn the king not
to believe a word of what the people were saying, for fear
he would become conceited. Used to his teasing by now,
Gilgamesh smiled at him with affection as they sat together,
comfortably reclining by the side of the pool.

"I almost wonder if we had anything to do with it, it
sounds so unfamiliar," he admitted. "Perhaps that is the way of
great deeds: Once accomplished, they are no longer ours, but
every man's, to do with as they please. They embellish the tale,
they garble it, they lengthen or shorten, until nothing but the
bare bones of the story remain true."

Enkidu nodded. "At least they have not entirely
eliminated either one of us from it yet. And one good thing
has come of our venture: You can have all the mighty cedars
that you need for building even greater temples and palaces
brought down the river. Your name will live long in the annals
of Uruk."

Gilgamesh stretched and clasped his hands behind his
head. "You know, now that I have you to keep me company,
we have made a name for ourselves with such an heroic deed,
and the building of the city is in a fair way to getting started, life
is truly become more enjoyable than I thought possible. And I
owe it all to you, my friend."

For once Enkidu felt the need to blush.

"Indeed you do not, my brother. What have I done?
You have attained all that you speak by yourself. You won the
contest that night I came to Uruk to challenge you, and thus
turned my heart toward you in friendship. It was your axe
that slew the mighty giant of the forest. In your wisdom it was

arranged to float the tall cedars along the course of the river. Without your vision, Uruk would be no grander than any other city of the plain. Without your eagerness for adventure, your life would be duller."

Gilgamesh nodded. "All you say has merit, and yet none of it would have come about but for your coming to seek me out. Were you not the man you are, no friendship would have grown between us, and I would not be the man I am today."

"When first you came to Uruk," Gilgamesh said, "I was but a headstrong youth. Now I am a man grown, for you have taught me to think before I act, and to consider well what I do. I have learned that even a king is no great thing in the eyes of his equals. Then there is the giant. Between you, you taught me to fear death and to love the life the gods have granted me, for I am also of the dust of the earth."

"All this," he continued, "I owe to you, though I suppose when one is both as strong as an ox and also as stubborn, new ways are not easily or speedily learned."

It was said with such unexpected humility that Enkidu was surprised. It seemed as though Gilgamesh had indeed learned much since his coming, little though he had guessed it. He smiled.

"If I have helped you to become a wiser and more responsible king, then I am content."

He shivered in the cool breeze from the river. The hot months were coming to an end, and an evening wind could be harsh on the exposed terrace. Gilgamesh noticed it and regarded him with fond concern.

"You are getting cold. I told you we should have taken

our meal below, after being out on the river all day."

Enkidu smiled. "It is just the wind. The rains of winter will soon be upon us, and my tunic is not as thick as your cloak. I shall have to ask your mother's women to weave me one just like it."

"Consider it done," Gilgamesh promised. "You will have it within the week."

Though the cloak was duly woven and delivered, Enkidu did not get to wear it. Two days after they sent the first set of barges north to fetch cedar trees to Uruk, what had seemed a slight chill turned into a feverish ague, and Enkidu had to stay abed in his rooms.

For a week Gilgamesh did not leave his side, having all meals brought in for the two of them, trying to tempt his friend to eat and keep up his strength. All the while the fever steadily mounted, and the priests and priestesses in the temples kept busy making intercession on Enkidu's behalf.

It was to no avail. The fevers of the river plain often attacked when the wet season first began. Though remedies abounded, few were strong enough to deal with an attack as powerful as the one that laid Enkidu low. He had little experience of sickness, but when his head and weak body were still burning on the eleventh day, he had no illusions about his fate.

When Gilgamesh returned from refilling the water-jug, it was to find silent tears coursing down his friend's sunken, flushed cheeks, a look of dread in his dark eyes.

"My brother, I am afraid I shall be leaving you," Enkidu

told him, his voice faint and hoarse, but resolute. "This is a journey I must go alone, and I fear it is a dark one. Will you stay with me until..." He could not bring himself to voice his great apprehension.

Gilgamesh sat on the bedside and took his burning hand in both of his, clasping it with an unwonted gentleness.

"Do not leave me yet," he pleaded. "How shall I go on without you? You have taught me to love another more than myself, the brother I never had, the equal I sought for so long. How can you die now, when we have accomplished so much, when the time has come for me to repay what you have done?"

Enkidu clutched at his hand as the breath caught in his throat. "Promise to remember me and all we did together, then I can always be close to you in your thoughts, and the darkness of the netherworld will seem lighter," he begged.

Gilgamesh nodded, anguish in his heart. "I myself will wear your great lion-skin, and the people of Uruk shall tell the stories of your coming and our battle with Humbaba every evening. I shall command a statue to be fashioned in your likeness as well, to be placed where I can see it daily."

The faintest hint of a smile rewarded Gilgamesh as Enkidu relaxed with a sigh.

"My thanks, brother. I shall sleep more soundly now."

He closed his eyes wearily. His grip on the king's hand gradually slackened. Gilgamesh listened to the shallow breathing, continuing to sit beside his friend, until sleep overwhelmed him as well and his head sank forward onto their joined hands.

In the course of the night, unnoticed even by the

slumbering king, Enkidu the wild man passed from sleep into death. His great heart stopped beating, his breath ceased. Far beyond the city walls, a lone wolf raised its head to the moon passing above the plains and howled.

The End

About the Author

Ms. Laurents was born in Krefeld, Germany, a mid-sized town on the lower Rhine. Her family moved to Oakland, California when she was almost eighteen. She attended U.C. Berkeley for her undergraduate studies and then went on to Law School, where she met her husband. After they were married in 1989, they lived in Florida, her husband's native state. More recently they moved to the state of Washington. Their three children and miniature dachshund keep them busy.

To my wonderful mother, Joy Marie Dunlap, my dearest friend and closest confidant, also a writer, for her love and support, and the inspiration and encouragement she gave me throughout my journey as a writer.

Imhotep
The Man Who Saved Civilization

by Jennaya Dunlap

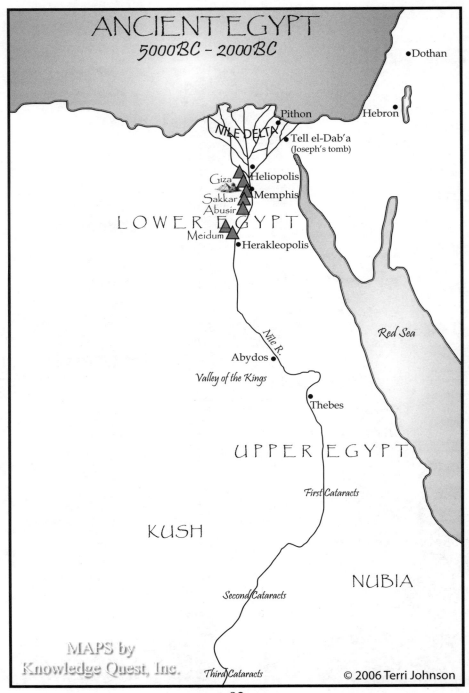

ANCIENT EGYPT
5000BC – 2000BC

•Dothan

Pithon
NILE DELTA
Tell el-Dab'a
(Joseph's tomb)
Hebron•

Giza Heliopolis
Sakkar Memphis
Abusir
LOWER EGYPT
Meidum
•Herakleopolis

Red Sea

Nile R.
Abydos•
Valley of the Kings
Thebes•

UPPER EGYPT

First Cataracts

KUSH

NUBIA

Second Cataracts

MAPS by
Knowledge Quest, Inc.
Third Cataracts
© 2006 Terri Johnson

4

Imhotep
The Man Who Saved Civilization

by Jennaya Dunlap

Around 1877, B.C., Egypt

ust swirled up from the parched ground beneath the men's sandaled feet and gathered into thick clouds. They covered their faces and trudged on, leading donkeys behind them. The journey had been long and exhausting, but now the gates of Egypt loomed only a short stretch away. Soon the brothers could rest their aching feet and find a place to sleep for the night, and most importantly, they could load their donkeys with sacks of food to take back to their starving families.

The famine had now lasted for almost a year. The skies were painfully blue, without a cloud in sight, and the land, once so rich and green, was brown and bare. Their supply of grain had dwindled away until it was almost gone, and the families faced starvation.

One day a stranger had passed by their tents, on his way home with grain-laden camels and exciting news. "There is plenty of food in Egypt," he told them. "People from all over the world are flocking there to buy corn from the great ruler, Imhotep. Look how much he has given me for my money!"

So the brothers had saddled their donkeys and set out immediately on the road to Egypt. And now, after so long, here they were. Throngs of people waited at the gate, speaking rapidly in many languages. The brothers pushed their way through the crowd until they reached the gate.

The gatekeeper pointed to the brothers and beckoned for them to step forward. "You! Come here!" They glanced at each other and stepped forward hesitantly.

"From where do you come?" the gatekeeper asked.

"The land of Canaan, sir," the oldest brother stepped up as a spokesman. "We are Hebrews."

"Your names?"

A young man at the gatekeeper's side wrote quickly on a tablet while the brothers answered. When they had finished, the gatekeeper swung open the heavy gate and stood aside for the brothers to pass through.

That evening in Imhotep's palace, Egypt

The heavy inner doors swung open and a servant crossed the long room. "My lord, the gatekeeper wishes to see you," he announced with a low bow. His words, addressed to Imhotep, echoed through the room. The high ceiling opened in a glass panel to admit sunlight during the day.

Imhotep stood up from his throne and handed a book of

figures back to the man at his side. "He can come in," he said simply.

The gatekeeper bowed to the ground before striding toward the throne. "My lord, I have brought you the list of names of those who have come through the Ten Gates of Egypt today."

"Thank you, Kazemde," Imhotep said as he took the book from the gatekeeper's arms. He scanned the pages of parchment with a quick eye. So many people, from so many nations – he knew that most of them had come to buy food.

His deputies sometimes offered to review the list of names for him, but he never let them. Every evening when he read over the names, he wondered if *they* had come yet, and every time he handed back the book with a sigh of disappointment. Perhaps they had some other source of food. But it had to run out sometime.

Tonight he skimmed the list of nations, reading the names of only those who had come from Canaan. Halfway down the fourth page his fingers halted at a scrawled entry. "Hebrews from Canaan." His heart skipped a beat and his shaking fingers traced the names of his brothers. Reuben, Simeon, Levi, Judah, Zebulun, Issachar, Dan, Gad, Asher and Naphtali. *They're here!*

He tried to hold back the excitement growing inside him. Now he had his chance to find out if they had changed. Would they recognize him?

How would he find them among the numerous grain shops he had set up around Egypt? He paced up and down next to his throne and prayed silently to God. A plan formed quickly in his mind – now he must work in haste to carry it out. He handed the book back to Kazemde and turned to his servant.

"Summon the grain distribution officers," he commanded. "I must speak to them at once." He watched as both men left the room, but his mind was far away. Had his brothers changed, or were they still hardened and cruel as they had been so many years ago when he had seen them last?

The dwellings of Israel and his sons, Canaan, about 1898 BC

"Joseph! Joseph!" His father's voice called his Hebrew name from within the tent. Joseph set down his little brother and stood up, brushing the dust off the back of his tunic.

"I'll finish the story later, Benjamin," he told his brother with a pat on his curly head and he hurried to Jacob's tent. When his eyes had adjusted to the dark interior, he saw his father's wrinkled face smiling at him.

"My son," he said and he took Joseph's hand into his. "Thank you for your faithfulness and obedience. You are my hope in my old age."

With a look of pleased satisfaction, Jacob draped a long tunic, dyed with many colors, about his son's shoulders.

Joseph's heart welled with happiness and he hugged his father and squeezed his work-worn hands. "You are welcome, my Father. It is my privilege to serve you." After a moment's silence as he inspected the new coat along the length of his arms, he lifted his eyes to meet his father's gaze. "But why have you given this to me, dear Father?"

"Am I not free to give a gift whenever I choose?" and his eyes twinkled. "But son, I called you for another purpose as well. I need you to go with your brothers to pasture the flocks," Jacob said. "They are leaving as soon as they have gathered their supplies."

He stood up with these words and lifted the flap of the tent. His hair shone gray and white in the sunlight that poured in. Joseph stepped to his father's side and accepted the staff he offered. Not far from the tents his ten older brothers had already gathered with the sheep and the donkeys that would carry their supplies. Before Joseph turned to leave, Jacob laid his hand on his shoulder.

"I trust you to do in my absence only what you would do in my sight," he said. His voice was firm and the solemn look he gave Joseph was mingled with a fond trust.

Joseph embraced his father and younger brother and hurried to join his brothers. They glared at him as he approached, noticing his fine new coat, but they said nothing. In fact, they said little to him all afternoon, but they jeered and talked loudly among themselves.

The sun passed its highest point and began to sink slowly toward the horizon. Judah and Levi chopped down branches and built a fire. While Asher prepared a stew, Joseph kneeled down by the fire to take the burrs out of the wool of a half-grown lamb. When he finished, he watched as it galloped to its mother's side.

"Those lambs are getting big now." Simeon was watching too, and now he spoke. He cast a warning look at Joseph as he continued. "We could sell them to some of the traders that have been passing through recently. They'd bring a good price and Father wouldn't have to know."

"No!" Joseph told him and he could feel heat rising to his cheeks. "You know that's wrong! Father forbade us to sell any of the sheep without his permission, especially not the lambs." He could feel his brothers' glares when he finished.

"Who cares? What can he do if he doesn't find out?" Simeon retorted with a scornful laugh. "Anyway, who are you to tell us what to do, *little* brother?"

"Simeon, he *will* tell on us," Judah warned, spitting in Joseph's direction. "You forget that Father sent him along with us so that he could be his eyes and ears." He lounged back on his cloak and chewed idly on a blade of wild grass.

Joseph scrambled to his feet and ran from the group. He fell to the ground under a clump of oaks some distance away and buried his face in his hands to pray. His father's parting words hung heavy in his mind – Jacob trusted him. How could he break that trust?

Back at the camp, his brothers' rowdy chatter ceased suddenly. They glared at him as he approached, but apparently had decided to let the matter of selling the sheep pass. He knew they could not trust him to keep their sinful secret. And they were right.

That night, Joseph dreamed that he was binding sheaves of wheat in the fields with his brothers. Suddenly his sheaf stood tall and straight, while his brothers' sheaves surrounded his and bowed to it. A few nights later, after they had returned home, he had another dream – the sun and moon and eleven stars bowed before him in the sky.

Both times, greatly puzzled, he told the dreams to his family. The first time, his brothers jeered. "So do you have the ambition to rule over us, little brother?" they taunted.

The second time, even his father was angry. "Do you actually want your mother and father and your brothers to bow before you?" he asked sternly. Joseph's brothers hated him for the dreams and teased him every chance they could get.

"Joseph!" Joseph set down the jug of water he carried on his shoulder and turned toward his father. Jacob waited by his tent until Joseph reached his side. Setting a hand on his shoulder, he asked, "You've heard, haven't you, that your brothers are pasturing the flocks in Shechem?"

Joseph nodded. His brothers had left several days earlier, without telling their father.

"Go to them and find out how they and the flocks are doing," Jacob continued, pausing for breath, "and bring me back a report." His gaze rested on Joseph's face for a moment before he turned to go inside the tent.

Joseph fastened a bag of provisions on his donkey's back and set out on his way. When he reached Shechem he looked anxiously for his brothers, but they were nowhere in sight. Dropping the donkey's rope, he fell to his knees in the middle of the stony field and prayed for God to show him where they were.

Before he had finished praying, a man appeared dressed in loose shepherd's garments and told him that his brothers had gone on to Dothan, further away. Joyously, he thanked the man and went on his way.

At last he could see his brothers' camp ahead. The sheep grazed quietly on the surrounding hillsides while his brothers gathered around a small fire. Trepidation was mixed with joy at finding them at last. They had barely spoken to him since he had shared his dreams, and when they did, their words were spiteful and cold. But perhaps this time it would be different.

His anticipation grew when several of his brothers came toward him as he approached. But he gasped when he saw the hateful expressions on their faces and the knife that Simeon brandished. He stepped back, but it was too late. His brothers surrounded him and some punched him while others tore off his colored tunic.

"Why? Why?" he cried out in shock. "Why are you doing this?"

"Kill him!" Levi yelled and Simeon raised his knife.

"Wait!" demanded Reuben, and his eyes flashed anger and terror. "He's your brother, your own flesh and blood! This act you intend to commit is wicked and detestable in the eyes of God! Stop, turn your hearts against this evil thing!"

The unspeakable terror in Joseph's heart gave way to faint hope at his brother's look as Simeon raised the knife again.

"You know how wrong this is," Reuben shouted, and he grabbed Simeon's arm. "Your conscience will forever be your enemy and will give you no peace if you let yourselves do this."

"Just kill him and get it over with," muttered some of the brothers.

"At least think of your father," Reuben continued with angry urgency. "If your hearts are so set against your brother, at least consider Father's grief and heartbreak when he hears." The brothers listened stonily before turning their murderous eyes on Joseph again. Joseph's eyes brimmed with hot tears and he held back sobs.

"At least do not shed his blood with your hands," Reuben said, taking the knife from his brother's hand. "Perhaps you can drop him down that pit over there instead and leave him to die there." With great difficulty, he persuaded them. Levi and Judah bound Joseph with a rope and Reuben let him down into the pit himself to prevent harm to him at his brothers' hands.

Joseph shook with sobs as he landed at the bottom of the deep earthen pit. The ground was muddy, but it was empty of water. Joseph tried to climb the wall, but the soft dirt gave way under his hands. Leaning against the wall, he cried out to his brothers and pled for their mercy, but to no avail. He knew they were nearby, for he heard their jeering voices as they gathered for a meal, but they didn't pay him any regard.

"What will we tell Father?" he heard one of them ask.

"We can say that a wild beast devoured him while he was in the wilderness," another answered. "We'll dip that wretched tunic in sheep's blood and show it to him as evidence."

Father! Pain shot through Joseph's heart at their words. How could his father bear it? He doubled over with heaving sobs. *Oh, God, how could you let this happen? How could they do this to our poor father?*

Hours passed and still Joseph remained in the pit. His screams and pleading words seemed to have no effect on his brothers' hard hearts. Before dusk he heard strange voices mixing with those of his brothers nearby the camp. In a few minutes, to his surprise, Judah leaned over the pit and lowered ropes.

"What's happening?" he asked as Judah hauled him onto the level ground above the pit. Strong hands pulled him roughly to his feet before his eyes adjusted to the light.

The heavy fragrance of myrrh and balm filled the air and a caravan of Ishmaelite traders waited nearby with camels laden with the treasure. The muscular caravan leader stood next to Joseph, bargaining loudly with his brothers.

"I'll give you fifteen shekels for him," he said.

"Twenty shekels," Simeon returned. "He's strong – you'll get a lot of work out of him." Suddenly it dawned on Joseph that he was being sold as a slave and his throat turned dry with horror.

"No, no!" He cried out. "Don't do this to me!" He looked around franticly for Reuben but he was nowhere in sight.

"Be grateful that I convinced them to do this instead of killing you," Judah retorted with an angry shove.

"Twenty shekels – it's a deal," the trader said and he handed the coins to Judah. "Tie him to the cart!" he commanded his men. "We have to get going again."

Joseph let out a cry of anguish when two men shackled his arms together with chains and dragged him to the cart. The caravan began to move amid clouds of dust and he took one hopeless look behind him at his triumphant brothers.

"Now let's see if your dreams happen now, slave!" Simeon taunted. A slave – in a few agonizing moments he had lost his freedom forever and now he was on his way to Egypt as the lowest of the low, to be bought as another man's property.

Joseph stepped out of the busy kitchen into the expansive dining room. The colorful mosaic tile under his sandaled feet reflected the coolness of the late morning air. The intricate glass chandeliers which hung from the high ceiling were lined with candles in preparation for the evening feast. The numerous long tables, likewise, were laid with white cloths and the finest dishes for the distinguished guests who would arrive later in the day.

Joseph was satisfied that his master's instructions concerning the feast were being carried out fully. He had just finished giving orders to the servants in the kitchen about the gourmet food and wine that were to be prepared. He hurried now to make sure that his master's chariot was ready as he had requested.

He remembered only too well the day he was dragged to the slave auction in the Egyptian capital. He had begged God as he stood, ill-treated and mocked on the slave block, to hear his pleas and preserve him even as a slave.

That day he had been bought by Potiphar, an important official whom he later learned was a steward in the court of the great Sesostris I, known as Pharaoh. He was brought home with several other slaves, but Potiphar took a liking to him and gave him special treatment. He educated him in the manner of a free man and gave him better food than most slaves received.

He tried his best to please his kind master and he worked hard in Potiphar's house. Potiphar was impressed with his honesty and faithfulness and soon he set him over his whole house. Joseph enjoyed the work and did his best at it. His heart ached for his father and his old home, but he knew God had brought him to Egypt for a reason.

One day, during a festival, when Potiphar and his men were away from the house, Potiphar's wife took advantage of being alone with Joseph. During previous months he had grown uncomfortable with how she looked at and talked to him. But this time she cornered him so he had no escape.

She tried to convince him to lie with her, but he refused. "I cannot betray the trust your husband has in me," he told her. "I will remain faithful to his trust and also to my God, in whose eyes it would be a very wicked thing."

Enraged, she grabbed onto his garments and tried to force him to lie with her, but he fled, slipping out of the garment held tight in her hands. To his horror, she screamed for the servants, crying out that he had tried to rape her. His heart leapt with anguish – how could she blame her own sin on him? Surely at least Potiphar would believe him after the faithfulness he had shown.

But when the master of the house returned home, she took him aside and told him that he had tried to force himself on her. Deceitfully she told him that when she had screamed and grabbed hold of him to restrain him, he had left his garment and fled to escape punishment.

"Seize him!" Potiphar shouted, and his voice shook with anger. "Throw him in the prison and let me never see his face again! I trusted him with everything in my house and he has betrayed me!"

Before Joseph could speak in his defense Potiphar's

guards seized him by the arms and dragged him out of the house. He struggled to keep up with the pace at which they pulled him down the wide streets. When he slowed down he was showered with blows. The night wind chilled him through his thin tunic and his sides were soon gripped with pain. A hollow, dazed feeling filled him with disbelief at the cruel accusations that had just been thrown at him.

Screams and the sounds of a whip met Joseph's ears at the gates of the prison. It was filthy inside and the inmates shouted and mocked each other. He was thrown into a dirty cell and the door was locked. He collapsed on the straw next to the dingy cot and raised his eyes toward heaven.

"My God, why have You let this happen to me? You know I'm innocent!" Tears fell fast from his eyes as he prayed these agonized words aloud.

In the days that followed, he felt God's peace flowing through him in spite of his terrible circumstances. The chief jailer, Nizam, saw his leadership abilities and faithfulness in the tasks he set for him, and he gave Joseph more freedom than the other prisoners. Before long, he was put in charge of the whole prison and he saw to it that conditions were improved for all the prisoners.

"Joseph," Nizam's voice sounded next to Joseph while he wrote in the prison record book. He looked up from his work and Nizam continued. "Two new prisoners have arrived – distinguished men from Pharaoh's court."

"Why are they here?" Joseph asked in surprise. He dipped his pen in ink and poised it to write.

"I'm not sure," Nizam answered. "They offended Pharaoh and he sent them here in anger. They had high positions – one was the king's chief cupbearer and the other was his chief baker."

Joseph wrote their names in the records of new prisoners while Nizam continued. "Joseph, I'm putting you in charge of them. Look after them and see that they get only the best treatment. If Pharaoh's anger eases and he asks for them, they must not have any bad reports to bring about their stay here."

"It will be as you say, sir," Joseph assured him without hesitation.

The two important men remained in the prison for several months. Joseph kept his promise and made sure they were treated well. One morning, when he made his usual rounds to check on all the prisoners, he noticed that both men looked anxious. Quickly he stepped into their cell.

"Is there something on your minds?" he wondered. "Both of you look miserable today."

The cupbearer raised his eyes to meet Joseph's. "If it weren't bad enough for the king to throw us in here and leave us to rot, we both were disturbed with dreams the same night and no one can interpret them for us."

"God gives us dreams and He also knows the interpretations of them," Joseph told him, sitting down nearby. "Tell me your dreams and perhaps He will reveal their meaning to me."

The cupbearer hesitated, but finally he began. "In my dream, I saw a grape vine with three branches. They budded and blossomed and clusters of grapes grew from the blossoms.

I had the Pharaoh's cup in my hand and I squeezed the grapes into it and put the cup in his hands."

As Joseph prayed the meaning became clear in his mind and he turned to the cupbearer. "The three branches are three days – in three days Pharaoh will lift up your head and restore you to your former office and you will once again put his cup in his hand."

The cupbearer's face lit up with joy and he leapt to his feet. Joseph laid a hand on his arm. "Please remember me when things go well with you and do me the kindness of mentioning me to Pharaoh, so I can get out of this place. I'm a Hebrew – I was kidnapped from the land of Canaan and brought here as a slave. Even here I did nothing to deserve being thrown in prison."

"I'll do what I can," the cupbearer promised absently. Joseph was tempted to press him further but no words came.

"Please listen to my dream," the chief baker entreated Joseph eagerly. "I dreamed that I had three baskets of white bread on my head and the top basket contained baked foods of all kinds for Pharaoh. But birds were eating from the basket. What do you think it means?"

Joseph hesitated, but finally began. "I'll not spare you the truth – the three baskets also represent three days..." Joseph paused and prayed for guidance, then continued. "In three days Pharaoh will lift up your head from you and hang you from a tree—"

"It can't be!" the chief baker shouted and his face turned pale with rage. But Joseph knew that what God had shown him was true. Three days later, on the Pharaoh's birthday, the interpretations he had given happened.

Two years later

The door of Joseph's cell burst open and several guards filed in. "Come quickly and make yourself presentable," they commanded him and they hurried him out of the cell.

"Why? What's happening?" Joseph asked, puzzled.

"You'll find out soon enough," the guards replied gruffly. "Hurry up!"

Joseph changed quickly into a new, clean tunic and shaved. *What will they do with me?* he wondered as he worked. But he felt God's peace over the situation and he pushed his apprehensions aside. When he had barely finished getting ready, the guards came for him.

They hurried him through the streets outside the prison and soon the palace loomed ahead. "The palace – what are we going there for?" Joseph wondered.

"Pharaoh wants to see you," a guard told him shortly.

Inside, he was led into a long, spacious room where the young king sat on his throne, surrounded by advisors and servants. Pharaoh rose from his throne when Joseph approached and took him by the hand.

"Young Hebrew, you have been brought from the prison because my cupbearer told me that you interpreted truthfully a dream he had," Pharaoh told him. "So is it true that you can interpret dreams?"

Joseph hesitated. "It is not me that has this ability – only God that knows the interpretations of dreams. But He reveals these things to me at times."

Pharaoh leaned forward eagerly. "I have had two terrible dreams, but none of my wise men and magicians can tell me what they mean. If you can give me the interpretations of my dreams, please do, but don't hide any of the meaning from me out of fear. I want the truth – I will not harm you."

"I will answer only what God shows me, nothing more," Joseph assured him.

"Good then," Pharaoh said, and he began. "I dreamed that I stood on the bank of the Nile River. Suddenly seven cows, fat and sleek, emerged from the river and grazed on the lush marsh grass. But then, seven more cows emerged, and they were ugly and gaunt, more so than I have ever seen."

He paused to glance at Joseph, who was deep in prayer. "These ugly, thin cows ate up the fat cows, yet they were just as thin and awful looking as before."

He paced up and down in front of his throne, highly disturbed. "I awoke then, but fell asleep again and had another terrible dream. Seven full, beautiful-looking ears of corn came up on one stalk, and suddenly seven more ears sprouted, but these were withered and wind-scorched. The thin, bad ears of corn ate up the first set."

Joseph turned his eyes sadly to meet Pharaoh's anxious gaze. "God has revealed to you what He is about to do. Both your dreams mean the same thing – the seven good cows and the seven good ears represent seven years of plenty, but the seven thin cows and seven ears of withered corn foretell seven years of famine."

Looking up, he saw that both Pharaoh and his advisors were listening intently to his words. "God has shown you what He intends to do, and He has given you two dreams to show you that the dream is sure. There will be seven years of unsurpassed abundance, but these will be followed by seven years of severe famine."

"But if this is what the dreams mean, how do we keep from starving during the famine?" Pharaoh asked, alarmed.

"Let the Pharaoh find a wise and discerning man and set him in charge of the land of Egypt," Joseph answered earnestly. "Let Pharaoh appoint overseers who will take a fifth of all the produce of Egypt during the seven abundant years and set it aside. Let them build storage places throughout the cities and store the grain there under guard. The food can be kept as a reserve when the famine begins so none of the people will starve during the seven terrible years."

The guards stepped toward Joseph when he finished speaking, but the Pharaoh's commanding voice stopped them. "No, leave him here!"

Joseph faced Pharaoh, his heart pounding within. Pharaoh strode down the steps from his throne. "It shall be as you have said," he told Joseph. "Does anyone know another man like this, who is bestowed with a divine spirit?" he asked, turning to his advisors. The men shook their heads solemnly.

"I have chosen you for this task," Pharaoh continued. He slipped off his signet ring. "Since your God has shown you all these things, there is no one as wise or discerning as you in all this land." Joseph's hand trembled so much that Pharaoh had to lift it himself to slip the ring on. He felt dazed, as if in a dream.

"I have set you over my own house – at your command

my people will do homage," Pharaoh told him. "Only by my throne will I be greater than you, for you now hold power greater than any other man except me." He put his gold necklace around Joseph's neck. "From this hour on you will be known as Zaphenath-Paneah, the Revealer of hidden things."

Tears streamed down Joseph's face as he thundered through the streets of the royal city in the king's second chariot. Hours earlier he had been in prison with no hope of redemption and now the people fell to their knees in the streets as he passed to pay homage to him as the second most powerful man in the world. Only through God's power could all of this have happened.

He was thirty years old that year – thirteen years had passed since his brothers sold him into slavery. His brothers – what would they think if they saw him now? Pharaoh gave him a palace of his own, complete with beautiful gardens.

He didn't stop to bask in his fame and glory, but set right to work to store away food for the famine. He ordered storage places to be built in every city and every year he sent men to set aside a fifth of all the produce and store it up in the nearest city. When he took the grain he made sure enough seed was leftover for the farmers to grow full crops the next year.

But only his overseers knew why he was doing it –he decided not to tell the people of Egypt lest they might panic. Meanwhile, Pharaoh gave him Asenath, the daughter of a great Egyptian priest, as his wife. Soon he had two sons, whom he named Manasseh and Ephraim.

The seven years of abundance slipped by one by one. One year, the ground turned parched and dusty and the crops

the farmers planted blew away in the dry winds. The famine had begun.

Frantically the people of Egypt gathered at the king's palace and begged him to give them food so they wouldn't starve. "Go to Joseph," he told them. "Do whatever he tells you to do."

Joseph was ready for that moment. He opened the store houses all over Egypt and the people flooded to them to buy grain. At first only the Egyptians came, but before long famished people from all over the known world heard that there was plenty of grain in Egypt. They flocked from all over the known world to buy the food.

Joseph became known as Imhotep, especially among the people of other lands. (Imhotep means "he comes in peace." Interestingly, "hotep" is linguistically very close to the name Joseph, which in Hebrew is "Yehoceph," and "Im" is similar to the Hebrew word for God, Elohim.)

From the first day of the famine onward he had watched for his brothers and now they were here. How would he find them? When the grain distribution officers arrived at the palace he gave them orders to close all the grain stores except one.

The following day, when he was at work in the single store that was open, he saw his brothers approaching in the waiting throng. The plan had worked! But how could he know if they had changed or if they were still as wicked as before?

When they reached him, they fell to their knees and prostrated themselves on the ground in front of him. Suddenly Joseph's dreams flashed before his eyes – they were coming true at that very moment!

The brothers trembled as they bowed before the great Imhotep. "You!" he shouted, and the brothers were startled and alarmed. He was a powerful man, clothed in garments of purple and blue linen. A golden crown topped his black Egyptian headdress. Never before had they seen a man of such wealth and power.

"Where have you come from?" Imhotep demanded through his interpreter. Reuben stepped forward and answered.

"No, you're spies!" Imhotep accused, shaking his forefinger at them. "You've come to check out the unprotected areas of the land!"

"No – your servants have come only to buy food!" Judah replied in agony. "We are all brothers, sons of one man. We are not spies."

In vain Judah explained that they were twelve brothers and all but one had traveled to Egypt to buy food. But, at Imhotep's command guards grabbed the brothers and carried them off to prison.

"You shall not leave until I see your youngest brother – it is the only way for me to know that you aren't spies!" the vizier thundered.

For three days the brothers remained in prison. At last the great vizier summoned them to come before him again and allowed them to buy grain to take home. But he warned them that one of the brothers must stay behind in prison until the youngest brother came with them to Egypt as proof of their story.

"This is punishment for what we did to Joseph," Simeon told his brothers in Hebrew.

"Yes," Levi agreed. "God has brought this on us because we didn't listen to his distress when he pleaded with us."

"I told you not to harm Joseph, remember?" Reuben whispered. "Now God is bringing reckoning for his blood." The brothers blushed with shame and looked at the ground.

"Take that one to prison," the vizier yelled, pointing to Simeon. Guards bound him and carried him off, while the brothers watched aghast. Imhotep turned to face the wall and when he returned to his throne his eyes were red.

Joseph paced up and down in his garden while his two sons climbed an old oak tree nearby. When would his brothers return, he wondered? He had ordered that their bags of money be returned in the sacks of grain before they left, and he wondered if they knew yet.

He had listened closely to his brothers' conversation in Hebrew and now he knew that they were sorry for what they had done to him. But was their repentance only because of their affliction? He wanted to be sure of their sincerity before he told them who he was.

Footsteps sounded behind him on the stone pathway. "Those Hebrews are back," the overseer told him in a low tone. Joseph followed him quickly to his waiting chariot.

"Is the other brother with them?" he asked.

"Yes," the overseer answered. Immediately Joseph gave orders to his stewards to prepare a feast at his palace and bring the men there to dine with him at noon. When they arrived he called them before him. He embraced Benjamin, overcome with emotion, and left the room to weep.

To their great astonishment he seated them around the feast table in the order of their births – from Reuben down to Benjamin. He served them all the richest food, but to Benjamin he gave five times as much.

Joseph gazed at the distant sunrise from the deserted throne room. The previous night he had commanded his stewards to place the money bags in his brothers' grain sacks again – but this time he also had them hide his cherished silver cup in Benjamin's sack.

The crunch of hoof beats and chariot wheels sounded on the road outside the palace. Finally his men had returned! He reached his throne the same moment the door flew open to admit his chief stewards. His brothers followed, guarded closely by armed men.

"We found the stolen cup," the steward said, holding the cup; "in Benjamin's sack."

"Why have you repaid evil for the good I have done for you?" Joseph yelled at his brothers. "Since it was found in Benjamin's sack, I will take him as a slave and the rest of you can return home."

Judah fell to his knees before Joseph. "No! No! Please don't do this to my father! He has already lost his most cherished son through our wickedness. If something were to happen to Benjamin our father would die of a broken heart."

Joseph turned away, wiping tears from his eyes as Judah continued. "When we left I promised my father that I would bring him back safe or sacrifice my own two sons – please don't do this to my father! Take me instead, and I will be your slave in his place."

Joseph felt a rush of tears and turned away, sobbing. "Leave this room, all of you!" he commanded his servants in a trembling voice. Alone with his brothers, he could restrain his sobs no longer and his shoulders heaved. He wept and wept and his whole body shook uncontrollably. The brothers stared in shock.

"I am Joseph!" he declared when he could finally speak again. "Is father still alive?"

His brothers stared, speechless, but he persisted. "Come closer – please – come, don't be afraid!" He threw his arms around each of them, sobbing, as they moved closer. "I'm your brother, Joseph, whom you sold into Egypt. I hid my identity because I wanted to find out if your hearts had changed."

He kissed Benjamin's forehead and turned to his brothers. "I tested you to find out how much you loved your brother, Benjamin. Now I know that your hearts have changed – that you would not betray Benjamin as you did to me long ago."

Several of his brothers began to weep when he said this. "God allowed this to happen for a purpose," he continued brokenly. "So that I could - could save people from dying of starvation." Great sobs shook his body again. The brothers wept and talked, for hours, holding each other close. Joseph embraced Benjamin especially, again and again.

Afterwards, they returned home to bring Jacob to Egypt, because Joseph wanted his whole family to live nearby, where they could be well-cared for during the remaining five years of the famine. He sent them home with wagons, laden with food and gifts.

All the people of Pharaoh's court went out with Joseph to greet his father when he arrived in Egypt. Joseph embraced his father with great emotion and tears of joy flowed again. Pharaoh allowed Joseph's family to live where they chose in the land of Goshen, near Joseph's palace, and he provided them with everything they needed.

The world continued to flock to Egypt for food as the famine grew worse. But their money was running out – all the money in Egypt and Canaan was now in Pharaoh's treasury. Joseph announced to the people that they could keep buying grain, in exchange for livestock.

But before the famine was over, all the livestock belonged to Pharaoh and there was none left to sell. Now the people began to sell their land in exchange for grain and the feudal system that had oppressed the Egyptian people for decades was abolished, for now all the land, except that of the priests, belonged to Pharaoh.

When the famine finally ended, Joseph distributed seed among the people. They could sow the land as they had before they sold it, under the condition that they give Pharaoh a fifth of the produce. Under his new law the land soon flourished and Egypt prospered again.

Epilogue

Jacob and his sons remained in Goshen until the ends of their lives, and for 400 years their descendants lived there. When Joseph died, after a long and full life, he requested that his bones be eventually transported back to Canaan. This request was fulfilled when the Israelites left Egypt after their long years in bondage.

Recent archeological findings revealed a palace near Goshen, built in a mix of Egyptian and Semitic styles such as Joseph would have done. Next to the spacious palace are elegant gardens and a small pyramid tomb.

The tomb shows signs of having been broken into – but the bones of whoever was buried there are missing, and the valuables that grave robbers would look for remain intact. If the tomb belonged to Joseph, this would make sense. Bricks were removed from the wall in a manner that suggests careful work, not vandalizing.

Near Lake Moeris, an artificial lake drained off the Nile, is a massive structure with twelve sections – quite possibly Joseph's grain storage headquarters. These and other archeological discoveries have caused many who formerly doubted the Biblical account of Joseph to believe in its accuracy.

About the author:

Jennaya Rose Dunlap wrote this story at the age of 16. Jennaya is homeschooled and the editor of a magazine for home schooled girls, ages 8 to 18, Roses In God's Garden, published by LightHome Ministries, www.lighthome.net. She is also the author of Against All Odds, a historical novel set in World War II  Poland under Nazi occupation, published as a serial story in her magazine. Jennaya enjoys writing and researching, drawing, singing and horseback riding. She enjoys spending time with her family on their acre beside a meadow with a mountain view, in California. She graduated from high school this year and plans to continue writing to publish.

To my precious first-born son: Jesse Ray. Remember when you were a little boy and I would wrap my arms around you and pray for you to grow "wise and strong and kind and good"? I am so thankful that God answered my prayers. Never forget your unique calling and the strength of God to make unpopular choices. I love you.

Daniel
Captive in Babylon

by Karla Akins

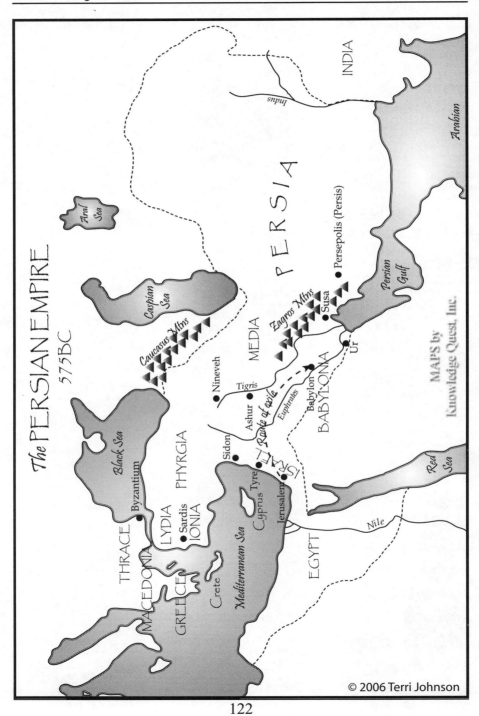

The PERSIAN EMPIRE
575BC

INDIA

Indus

Arabian

PERSIA

Aral Sea

Persepolis (Persis)

Caspian Sea

Persian Gulf

Susa

Caucasus Mtns

Zagros Mtns

MEDIA

Nineveh

Tigris

Ur

Ashur

Route of exile

Babylon

BABYLONIA

Euphrates

Black Sea

Byzantium

PHYRGIA

Sidon

ISRAEL

LYDIA

Sardis

IONIA

Cyprus

Tyre

Jerusalem

Red Sea

THRACE

MACEDONIA

GREECE

Crete

Mediterranean Sea

EGYPT

Nile

MAPS by
Knowledge Quest, Inc.

© 2006 Terri Johnson

5
Daniel
Captive in Babylon

by Karla Akins

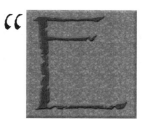

"Eyes up here, Daniel," Jeremiah said tapping the table in front of him. "Focus on your studies. Tell me again the words of our father Abraham when the Lord spoke to him at Ur?"

14-year old Daniel was distracted. He was normally an attentive student, but the siege of the Babylonian army outside the city walls of Jerusalem, and the rumors that the siege ramps were nearly complete, troubled him. For months he had watched the Babylonians outside the city walls as they constructed six-wheel battering rams, siege machines and wall-high towers. There were soldiers on Mt. Olivet spying on the city, and his father had seen Nebuchadnezzar's chariot patrolling his army. Men on magnificent horses rode up and down the walls shouting orders. Knowing all these things made it difficult for the young Daniel to concentrate.

"Thompf, Thompf, Thompf." What was that sound that made the ground shake and the tables rattle?

Before Daniel could answer Jeremiah's[1] question, screams exploded into the little classroom from outside the prophet's house. Daniel and his friends looked imploringly at their teacher. He nodded.

"Go," he said, waving his arm at the door, "Go to your fathers at the walls. Go to your families. God is with you and will deliver you! Remember that. Go!"

"Thompf, Thompf, Thompf."

The unmistakable sounds of battering rams pounding down the doors at the gates of the city echoed so loudly that Daniel could feel them in his chest.

The boys threw down their stone tablets and honey jars and ran as fast as they could into the cobbled streets of Jerusalem.

"Daniel!" Mishael gasped, "The Babylonians are ruthless! We will die!" The boys ran in tandem as fast as their legs could carry back to the neighborhood wall where their fathers met with the other nobles of the land. They were all afraid, but only Mishael was going to admit it.

"Hush, Mishael," his friend Azariah scolded. "From your mouth to God's ears – where is your faith?"

"Thompf, Thompf, Thompf . . ."

---

[1] We don't know that the Prophet Jeremiah was Daniel's teacher, but they did live at the same time. Jeremiah was about 25 years older than Daniel.

"Be patient with him, Azariah," Hananiah said. "He is right. The Babylonians are cruel. They skin their captives alive and drive them naked from their cities. But we must have faith, Mishael. Isn't that right Daniel?"

"Yes, for Yahweh will never leave us nor forsake us," he said. "We will do well to remember our studies and to hide the words of God in our heart."

"Agreed," Azariah said. All the young men nodded as they turned the corner. They stopped and looked longingly at one another before parting. Would they ever see one another again? Would they live or die? Many questions troubled their hearts but they were determined to trust Yahweh-Nissi – "The Lord Our Banner." He would protect them in this battle.

"Thompf, Thompf, Thompf . . ."

"Remember!" Daniel shouted as he ran away. "Remember all you have learned! Remember Yahweh[2] will deliver you!"

"Shalom Alechim! (Peace be with you!)," they cried to one another as each went their own way.

Daniel ran through the city, jumping over garbage and sick people lying in the streets. The stench was nearly unbearable and Daniel strained to ignore it. For weeks the Babylonians had laid siege to their fair city. And now - could it really be that Jerusalem, the place where God had put His name - would be defeated today? Yes, it was indeed possible. For his own teacher, Jeremiah the prophet, had told them the words of the Lord:

---

[2] Yahweh means "I am eternal." It is God's personal Name.

"Behold, I will send and take all the families of the north, saith the LORD, and Nebuchadnezzar the king of Babylon, my servant, and will bring them against this land, and against the inhabitants thereof, and against all these nations round about, and will utterly destroy them, and make them an astonishment, and an hissing, and perpetual desolations."[3]

"Thompf, Thompf, Thompf. . ." the sound was deafening as he drew closer to the city wall. The shouts of men around the tops of the walls, and the smoke coming from the cities burning nearby, made it hard for Daniel to find his father. Men stood on the tops of the city walls, throwing rocks and hot liquid onto the Babylonians below. But the arrows, sling-stones and huge rocks from the catapults continued to barrage the city walls. Hebrew men fell from the walls screaming, and each man that died weakened Jerusalem's defenses.

The Babylonian bowmen were skilled and fierce warriors because of their practice in battles with the Assyrians. They were fearsome to the Israelites, with their tunics of scale armor and helmets. Their composite bows allowed them to strike targets from a long range. This meant that the strong-armed bowmen were the dominant force of their army.

"Thompf, Thompf, Thompf. . ."

Suddenly there was deathly silence. All at once the fighting stopped. The battering ram ceased to pound against the thick cedar gates.

Daniel spotted his father and ran up the steps and a ladder to meet him. He looked out of place in his noble garb

---

[3] Jeremiah 25:9

next to the soldiers and commoners of the city. His father saw him and motioned him away.

"Run, my son! Go tell your mother and sisters that King Jehoiachim has surrendered to the Babylonians! As a condition of the surrender, Nebuchadnezzar will take 10,000 Israelites as hostages! Hurry, Daniel – go!"

Without saying a word, Daniel jumped from the ladder and ran toward home. It was up to him now to protect his family. His father was busy advising the military leaders and seeking counsel among the other nobles of Judah.

Daniel ran, the muscles in his legs straining as he mounted the steep steps of the city leading to his palace home. His lungs burned as he gasped for air. His creamy brown skin shone in the sunlight, and his silky black hair glistened with perspiration.

But it was too late. Just as he reached the threshold of his palace home, the door was forced open revealing a fierce looking Babylonian with three others like him. They grabbed Daniel, turning him around, and forced him in the opposite direction.

~~~

"Take these four," the chief of the eunuchs pointed to Daniel and his friends. "They are strong, fine to look at, and able to read. The king will want them to train as his advisors."

Daniel and his three friends were shackled and forced into line with other young men from noble families. Tears hung on his eyelashes as he thought about his family. Would he ever see his mother again? What would happen to his sisters? Where was his beloved father? He shuddered and tried desperately not to think about it.

"O Lord my God, in thee do I put my trust: save me from all them that persecute me, and deliver me."[4]

Suddenly Daniel was shoved from behind.

"Move! Forward!" The soldiers pushed and prodded their captives, moving them forward into the desert sun.

A sea of young men and women moved away from Jerusalem and into the desert of Sinai toward Babylon. Only the most educated, healthy, beautiful, talented and noble citizens were taken prisoners. The poor, sick, elderly and farmers were left behind – this time. It would take Nebuchadnezzar two more trips to Jerusalem to destroy the holy city completely.

Daniel was worried about Jeremiah. Had he been able to hide some of the temple vessels? He noticed that while some of the temple vessels were put into sacks carried by the Babylonian military leaders, he was sure they weren't all stolen. There were too few sacks full. He thanked God that somehow they had not managed to steal the Ark of the Covenant. Did Jeremiah have something to do with that? He hoped his teacher was safe and unharmed.

Daniel loved the temple of Jerusalem! It gleamed in the sun and its gold doors shone with splendor. He had never gotten to see inside the Holy Place, but Jeremiah had told him about what was inside. Jeremiah had taught Daniel to love the Temple of the One True God.

Daniel's heart broke as he watched soldiers forcing

---

[4] Psalm 7:1

some of the Israelite prisoners to march with millstones upon their backs. The stones tore at their bare skin and weighed the young men down in the hot desert sands. The more difficult and strong-willed prisoners were shackled with their elbows together and heavy chains around their necks. They were unable to swat away the flies that bit at the scratches on their legs and arms and face.

"Preserve me, O God: for in thee do I put my trust." Daniel's whispered words of King David comforted him, but he also meant them from his heart as a prayer.

Daniel whispered the prayer over and over again as he walked under the blazing sun in the hot desert sands. He was thirsty and hungry and tired.

"Keep them moving!" the soldiers yelled. "Do not let them stop and pray! They must not rest until they reach the Euphrates!"

For over 800 miles, the Israelites were herded like animals to Babylon. They were humiliated by the soldiers' mocking. It was a horrible time of hunger and weakness. But Daniel persevered because of what his parents taught him.

"Remember the books of Moses, Daniel, remember the songs of King David, my son..."

His mother's words rang in his ears. He sang in his heart to the Lord in spite of the pain to keep hate from welling up in his heart toward his captors. He would not – he could not – become as they were. And only forgiveness would keep bitterness from his heart and lips.

"The LORD is my light and my salvation; whom shall I fear?" he

whispered to His God, "the LORD is the strength of my life; of whom shall I be afraid?"[5]

"If only our people had paid attention to the prophet Jeremiah," he groaned with each heavy step. "If only they had obeyed God – this would not have happened."

He looked ahead of him toward the strongest Hebrew warriors carrying heavy trunks of cedar trees Nebuchadnezzar had taken from Lebanon to use in building the city of Babylon. Nebuchadnezzar was obsessed with building Babylon into a city full of ziggurats and walls to the god Marduk. As strong as these soldiers were, their muscles strained to keep the cedars in their arms.

Behind Daniel came the roar of lions and the trumpeting of elephants. Nebuchadnezzar collected animals the same as he collected people.

Day after day, the children of Israel journeyed in great despair and discomfort to the wicked city of Babylon. They were not allowed to rest during the hours of their journey until they reached the river Euphrates. Once there, the king held a big feast on his ship. But he didn't invite the Hebrew people to join him. While they lay chained and starving on the shore of the river, he ate every delicacy to his heart's delight.

"Bring those Hebrew temple musicians!" he roared. "They shall play for the king!"

The temple musicians were brought to the king but they refused to play for him.

---

[5] Psalm 27:1

"We would rather bite off our fingers first," they cried, "than to play our sacred music in honor of your false gods!" Nebuchadnezzar ordered them to be executed.

Day after day, week after week, month after month, Daniel and his people traveled to Babylon. They were burned from the sun and weak with hunger. Finally, one day, Daniel saw something glistening in the distance. It looked like a jewel in the sand – it was magnificent and beautiful. What was it?

As they drew closer, he blinked his eyes to make sure he was really seeing the beautiful blue and gold archway gleaming in the sun. It was extraordinary.

"Behold the gate of Ishtar!" Nebuchadnezzar cried out in a booming voice. "Behold Babylon in all her glorious splendor!"[6]

The haughty king roared with laughter. Daniel stole a look at Nebuchadnezzar and was startled to realize that this great king, who caused all the Israelites to tremble, was but a young man in his early twenties! How could this young man bring such terror to the entire world?

He looked from the king back to the enormous arch before them on the other side of a large moat that surrounded the city. The arch was magnificently huge and made of glazed blue brick. Some of the bricks were molded so that when they were put together they made pictures of golden lions and dragons and bulls. Daniel couldn't help but notice the craftsmanship and beauty of the gate as he traveled under

---

[6] The gate of Ishtar probably wasn't built until after Daniel had lived in Babylon a few years.

it. The mythical dragons of Marduk gleamed on the walls, in bronze and gold, with a scaly body, serpent's head, and viper's horns. It had front feet like a cat's and the hind feet were talons of a large bird. Its tail was like a scorpion's. Marduk was the chief god of Babylon. And Ishtar, whom the gate was dedicated to, was the goddess of love and war.

Nebuchadnezzar bellowed out the inscription on the Ishtar gate:

"Nebuchadnezzar, King of Babylon, the faithful prince appointed by the will of Marduk, the highest of princely princes, beloved of Nabu, of prudent counsel, who has learned to embrace wisdom, who fathomed their divine being and reveres their majesty, the untiring governor, who always takes to heart the care of the cult of Esagila and Ezida and is constantly concerned with the well-being of Babylon and Borsippa, the wise, the humble, the caretaker of Esagila and Ezida, the firstborn son of Nabopolassar, the King of Babylon.

"Both gate entrances of Imgu-Ellil and Nemetti-Ellil following the filling of the street from Babylon had become increasingly lower. Therefore, I pulled down these gates and laid their foundations at the water table with asphalt and bricks and had them made of bricks with blue stone on which wonderful bulls and dragons were depicted. I covered their roofs by laying majestic cedars length-wise over them. I hung doors of cedar adorned with bronze at all the gate openings. I placed wild bulls and ferocious dragons in the gateways and thus adorned them with luxurious splendor so that people might gaze on them in wonder.

"I let the temple of Esiskursiskur (the highest festival house of Marduk, the Lord of God's a place of joy and celebration for the major and minor gods) be built firm like a mountain in the precinct of Babylon of asphalt and fired bricks."[7]

When the arrogant Nebuchadnezzar was finished reading the inscription, he marched his captives down the street called "The Sacred Way".

It seemed that they marched down countless streets lined with altars and little shrines made to the many different gods and goddesses of Babylon. They passed under eight massive gates that led to the middle of the city, as well as countless brass ones.

Finally, Nebuchadnezzar stopped the marching of the prisoners by the east bank of the Euphrates that ran through the middle of the city. There stood an enormous seven-story building called "Etemenanki, House of the platform of Heaven and Earth."

"Is this the tower of Babel, Daniel?" Azariah asked.

"I don't know - I wish Jeremiah were here to tell us," Daniel whispered. He scanned the 300 feet of the Ziggurat, up to the temple at its peak. A wide staircase wound up its side to each level. Hananiah wanted to climb to the top, not to worship Marduk, but to see the spectacular view.

Daniel looked south from the "Etemenanki" and could see the 'House of the Raised Head,' the shrine of the city-god

---

[7] www.bible-history.com/babylonia/BabyloniaThe_Ishtar_Gate.htm

Marduk, also called Bel, 'The Lord.' There were also shrines
to Marduk's son Nabu and other gods and goddesses there.
Daniel wondered if there weren't thousands of them. He
thought he had counted at least 180 altars to Ishtar alone.

"I am glad I have only One True God to worship," he
said to himself. "I would tire of keeping track of as many gods
as these."

It was getting dark, and off in the distance Daniel saw
what he thought looked like a mountain, but his eyes were
growing dim, and he was weak from hunger. Daniel whispered
a prayer that God would grant him a place to rest very soon
– because he didn't think he would be able to stand for much
longer.

"Ashpenaz!" the king bellowed.

"Yes, O Great One!" A large dark man dressed in a
long white linen tunic to the feet, bowed to the king. His thick
wavy black hair flowed over the back of his wool robe, and
his perfectly combed beard rested on his chest. Daniel fought
not to sneeze because of the thick perfume that emanated from
him. He, as well as other officials, carried a walking stick,
with fancily carved heads. The seals that he used to seal the
clay envelopes of his clay letters, dangled from his girdle and
jangled as he walked.

"What is your pleasure, sire?"

"Ashpenaz, you are to inspect these foul humans I have
brought from Jerusalem and pick out the youngest men in
whom there are no blemishes. Choose only the handsomest and
those skillful in all wisdom."

"Yes, your highness."

"And cunning in knowledge." The king put his hand on his chin, and paused.

"And understanding science, and such as have the ability in them to stand in the king's palace…and, they shall be taught the learning and the tongue of the Chaldeans!"

"Those are large goals, sire."

"But worthy goals -- especially with the best and brightest. Now, go find them. Go!"

~~~~

Daniel was starving. Ashpenaz, the prince of the eunuchs, put Melzar in charge of Daniel and his three friends. They had been bathed and given beautiful new clothes. But it didn't stop the pangs of hunger pinching in their stomachs.

"Now," Ashpenaz said. "You have new clothes. You need new names to go with them. Daniel, you are now Belteshazzar. Hananiah, you are Shadrach. Mishael, Meshach is a good name for you, and Azariah, I hereby name you Abednego."

The boys cringed. Their Hebrew names were given to them for sacred reasons. But they knew that this was Nebuchadnezzar's way of taking ownership of them. They also knew in their hearts that they were not what someone else said they were – they were who God said they were.

"Come with me," Melzar said. "I have a surprise for you."

They followed Melzar into another room where a table had been set with the king's meat and wine. The boys' mouths watered and the pinching in their stomachs became even worse. The delicious aromas of mutton and beef wafted into their nostrils making their mouths water. There were many varieties of fish and poultry, too. The young men's hungry eyes surveyed the table laden with barley cakes sweetened with date-syrup, grapes, apricots, pomegranates, figs, lettuces, radishes, onions, garlic, and even gherkins of various kinds. There was beer and wine to drink. But as thirsty and hungry as Daniel was, he knew he would not be able to eat the food offered to them.

"Everyday you shall eat and drink the daily provision of the king's meat and wine. After three years, you will be strong and healthy enough to stand before the king!"

Suddenly, Daniel purposed in his heart that he would not defile himself with food that had been offered to idols or that he was not supposed to eat because of the Hebrew laws. He was hungry, but he was hungrier for God's favor in his life, and wanted more than anything to please Him.

"Melzar," Daniel said softly.

"Yes, young Belteshazzar, what is it?"

"I cannot eat the meat and food or drink the beer and wine that is offered here."

"What do you mean you can't eat it? You are starving and you stand there and dare to tell me you refuse to eat this food that has been so generously provided to your table?"

"I am most appreciative, sire, I do not mean to offend. But if we could just have some vegetables and water. . ."

Melzar liked this young man, Daniel. For reasons he couldn't quite put his finger on, he had a tender spot in his heart for this Hebrew.

"Daniel, I have grown quite fond of you these past few

weeks. But I am afraid that the king will not be pleased if you refuse to eat the meat he has required and drink his beer. If you don't eat, you will not be healthy, and then the king will surely have my head! Now, eat! It is the king's pleasure!"

"Please, Melzar, just let us try it for ten days. Just give us vegetables – and beans and peas – and water to drink. And then compare us in ten days to the other children who eat all of the king's meat. And if they are healthier than we are, then you can deal with us as you wish."

Melzar looked at Daniel and saw the young man's sincerity. Perhaps he knew something he didn't. He reluctantly agreed.

"Remove the king's food!" he said. "And give these young men pulse - peas, beans, legumes, herbs and vegetables - to eat for ten days."

Ten days later, Daniel and his three friends were not only healthier, but they were also ten times better in wisdom and understanding than all the magicians and astrologers in the kingdom!

~~~~~

The king wanted to have advisors who were wise and clever and good at science. Daniel had been one of Jeremiah's brightest pupils, and he was one of the brightest in Babylon, as well.

Daniel had always enjoyed learning, but he was learning things now that he had never gotten to learn before. He had been in Babylon for a year. While he still missed his father and mother and sisters, he did enjoy his studies, and he had not forgotten to pray to the One True God and study His Word.

137

He went to tablet school every day and was grateful to get to work hard at his studies. Other Hebrew teenagers had been made slave laborers. The Babylonian students were those of wealthy families. Even some girls from these families were allowed to study.

It was sometimes tedious and arduous work, but Daniel and his three friends from Jerusalem learned ten times faster than the other students. He spent hours writing in cuneiform into clay tablets. Hour after hour he copied from other clay tablets and helped the younger students with theirs.

"Look what I wrote, Belteshazzar!"

Young Basha proudly held out his clay tablet for Daniel to see.

"Well done, young scribe," Daniel said. "Now read it to me as you will read it to your father."

Basha smiled and read aloud what he had written:

"I went to the tablet house; ...
I read out my tablet, ate my lunch,
Prepared my (fresh) tablet, inscribed it (and) finished it...
When the tablet house was dismissed, I went home.
I entered (my) house.
My father was sitting there.
I read over my tablet to him and he was pleased..."[8]

Daniel smiled and patted the young boy on the head. "You are already an expert scribe. Indeed your father will be

---

[8] Taken from an actual tablet school tablet (www.aina.org).

proud. Now, get busy at your mathematics before The Expert canes you!"

Basha smiled up at his "Big Brother." Older students were given younger students to help guide and mentor, and Basha clearly admired Daniel and his wisdom.

Daniel scowled at his algebra studies. The base 60 system of the Babylonians was a challenge, but he enjoyed it immensely. Since arriving in Babylon he had become acquainted with the 360-degree circle, and the 60-minute hour. He had also learned how to predict eclipses of the sun and moon,[9] and do fractions, squares and square roots.

Daniel pressed his stylus into wet clay to make the cuneiform shapes to form his numbers. For the number ten, he pressed a wedge into the clay pointing to the left. For numbers less than ten he placed the wedges pointing down. And for all numbers less than 60 he combined the symbols of 1 and 10. There was no symbol for zero, so Daniel left a space.

Daniel was tireless in his studies. Though his neck ached and his fingers became sore from pressing the stylus into the clay hour after hour, he relished learning all the new and fascinating things at his school. He copied and memorized both textbooks and dictionaries containing long lists of words and phrases. He wrote and memorized the names of animals, birds, trees, countries, insects, cities, villages and minerals. He

---

[9] There is also a belief among the Hebrews that the signs and their constellations, in their purest form, foretold the coming of the Messiah, and later became corrupted within pagan cultures. Some believe Daniel recorded the position the stars would shine at the birth of Christ, and it was his writings that led the Magi to worship Him.

had copied and memorized a vast array of mathematical tables and problems. He copied the library's myths, epics, proverbs, essays and lamentations. And even though he became well versed in all of Babylonian knowledge and culture, he never forgot where he came from or whom he served. He also studied God's Holy Word and continued to practice his Aramaic and Hebrew.[10]

Every day after he was finished with his schoolwork, he placed his clay tablets in the sun and let them bake. Then, he would walk back to his room at the palace, kneel at the window facing Jerusalem, and lifting his hands toward heaven, he would pray. Though his mind was overflowing with knowledge, more than anything else, he longed for the wisdom of God.

From his balcony, Daniel could see the ancient, glorious city of Babylon. Its beauty did not move him because of his faith. However, he understood why it held visitors' awe and wonder. Babylon's splendor was truly breathtaking to behold.

The walls alone were an engineering feat. The outer walls were 56 miles in length, 320 feet high and 80 feet thick: wide enough to allow a four-horse chariot to turn on. Inside the walls were more strong walls surrounding fortresses and temples. These buildings contained immense statues of solid gold. Rising above the entire city was the enormous temple to the god Marduk. The Babylonians thought it reached to the heavens, but Daniel knew better.

In spite of being surrounded with all the beauty and splendor of false gods, riches and all the temptations of the

---

[10] The book of Daniel in the Bible was written in both Aramaic and Hebrew.

world, Daniel never turned his back on the God of his parents. He could have been, or done, anything he wanted in Babylon. Instead, he chose to serve the One True God: Yahweh.

"I am nothing without You, Lord," he whispered. "Gold cannot hear my prayers. Marduk cannot weep with me for my people. Only You, O Lord, are my rock and my salvation. Only in You will I put my trust!"

~~~~

Years passed and Daniel became one of the king's most trusted advisors. He won the king's favor by his hard study and great wisdom and Daniel always gave God the glory. He never became proud and he never took credit for any of his success.

Jerusalem, where he had once been free to worship God without fear of harm, was still in trouble. Nebuchadnezzar had placed another king over Judah – Jehoiachin, the son of Jehoiachim – but he was not cooperating with Nebuchadnezzar's wishes.

Daniel loved Jerusalem and the life he had lived there. He longed for the days he sat at his mother's table eating her food and hearing the chatter of his family. He yearned to see Jeremiah's face again and sit in Hebrew school, dipping his fingers into honey to form the letters of the Hebrew alphabet.

"How sweet are thy words unto my taste! yea, sweeter than honey to my mouth!"[11] Daniel whispered the words of King David to himself, and remembered his love for learning God's words.

---

[11] Psalm 119:103

There were many things about Babylon that were so breathtakingly beautiful on the surface that the world was in awe of the great kingdom. But for Daniel, nothing would ever compare to the beauty of his beloved Jerusalem and the Temple of God.

Still, there was no denying that Babylon was full of many things to please the eye. Even Daniel enjoyed a paradise in the middle of the desert that Nebuchadnezzar had created for his young bride, Amytis. People called it "The Hanging Garden."

Nebuchadnezzar's wife was from Media and she missed the beautiful mountains of her homeland. There were no mountains in Babylon,[12] so he decided to build her a mountain himself. He fashioned a multi-story garden with an irrigation system that kept it continually watered. The garden did not really hang, but the roots of palm trees and other plants clung to the edges of terraces and their branches hung downward. The leaves, fruits and flowers of various plants and vines spilled over the edges of each level creating the look and feel of a hanging garden. From afar, it really did look like a beautiful mountain.

It was a haven for colorful birds that made their homes there: Indian Rollers, Hoopoes, and colorful varieties of Kingfishers and Trogans, who loved the lush foliage and hanging trees. There was so much blue, red and gold in these various birds, Daniel couldn't help but wonder if they had inspired Nebuchadnezzar when he designed the bright enamel-

---

[12] Modern-day Iraq

glazed walls of Babylon.

Various exotic breeds of animals - monkeys, lizards and other reptiles - roamed the gardens freely. Baby elephants, ostriches, and other animals from all over the empire made their home in the beautiful garden. The scents that rose from the garden's fauna were sweet and comforting. The sounds of the water wheels and the songs of the birds made it a gloriously peaceful haven from the busy streets below it. Once inside the garden's walls, it was like entering an entirely different world.

"Nebuchadnezzar thinks this is all his doing alone," Daniel thought when he saw the garden for the first time. "But only God could put such color in a Kingfisher and the hue on a rose."

"Even mountains are God's idea." Daniel mused. *"Before the mountains were brought forth, or ever thou hadst formed the earth and the world, even from everlasting to everlasting, thou art God."*[13]

Daniel had stopped by the garden to watch the birds and had caught a glimpse of Amytis playing with her pet monkeys from China when a messenger came to him.

"The king is having all the wise men in the kingdom murdered! You must hide!"

But before the messenger could take Daniel to safety, the king's captain, Arioch, and his soldiers approached.

"Seize him! By order of the king!"

"What have I done?" Daniel asked.

"The king has ordered all of his wise men to be killed because they cannot tell him what he dreamed and the meaning

---

[13] Psalm 90:2

of his dream!"

"Wait!" Daniel said. "Let me ask the king for mercy and give my God time to give me the interpretation of his dream."

After Daniel talked to the king, he went to his friends, Hananiah, Mishael, and Azariah. They prayed and asked God for the meaning of the dream. And that night, God gave Daniel the meaning. Oh, how Daniel blessed God for this miracle!

"Blessed be the name of God for ever and ever:
for wisdom and might are his: And he changeth the times and the
seasons: he removeth kings, and setteth up kings: he giveth wisdom
unto the wise, and knowledge to them that know understanding:
He revealeth the deep and secret things: he knoweth what is in the
darkness, and the light dwelleth with him. I thank thee, and praise
thee, O thou God of my fathers, who hast given me wisdom and might,
and hast made known unto me now what we desired of thee: for thou
hast now made known unto us the king's matter."[14]

"Arioch!" Daniel shouted. "Do not destroy the wise men of Babylon! Bring me before the king!"

"You can tell me my dream and its interpretation?" the king asked Daniel when he approached. The king was haggard and pale. He hadn't slept for days.

"O King, the secret you want revealed no wise man can show you. But I serve a God that reveals secrets, and it is He who will show you what is going to happen in the future! It is important to understand that it is not me who is wise. It is God

---

[14] Daniel 2:20:23

that has revealed this secret."

"Go on," Nebuchadnezzar said.

"O king, in your dream was a huge, frightening image. It had a head of gold, breast and arms of silver, belly and thighs of brass, legs of iron and feet of iron and clay. As you were looking at this image a huge stone crashed down on the feet and broke them into pieces. Even the iron, clay, brass and silver were broken and became chaff and the wind carried them away."

"Yes! Yes!" the king was sitting on the edge of his seat. This young Judaean had looked into the secrets of the night and was telling him the dream!

"The stone that smote the image became a great mountain, and filled the whole earth," Daniel said.

"But what does it mean?" Nebuchadnezzar cried, his fist in the air.

"O king, God has given you this kingdom, and you are the head of gold. But after your kingdom another kingdom will arise that is not as great as yours. A third kingdom, the brass, will rule over all the earth after the silver one. The fourth kingdom will be strong as iron. And the feet and toes, part of potters' clay and part of iron – that kingdom will be divided. It will be partly strong and partly weak. And in the days of this kingdom, the God of heaven will set up a kingdom that will last forever. This is the interpretation and this is what is going to happen."

"Your God *is* a God of gods, and a Lord of kings, and a revealer of secrets!" The king said, leaping from his chair. "I hereby make you ruler over the whole province of Babylon.

You are to be chief of the governors and of all the wise men of Babylon!"

"O King," Daniel said. "If it please you, I have three friends upon whose help and wisdom I depend. I will need them to aid me in this great responsibility."

"Agreed," the king said. "But YOU will sit in the gate of the king."

From that time on, Nebuchadnezzar enjoyed the company of Daniel and called on him often for advice in running the kingdom of Babylon.

But Nebuchadnezzar didn't remember the greatness of Daniel's God for long. In fact, he made a huge image of gold and commanded everyone in Babylon to bow to it every time the band played. And anyone who didn't worship it would be cast into a burning fiery furnace.

He sent invitations to all the kingdom's rulers to come to the dedication of the image. It was a big party with dancers, singers and musicians of all kinds. Everyone in the kingdom came, and when the music sounded, they all bowed to the image. But there were some Chaldeans who noticed that Daniel's friends, Shadrach, Meshach and Abed-nego weren't bowing and some of the king's wise men made sure the king knew it.

"O King!"

"What is it?"

"Not everyone is bowing! Look!"

Nebuchadnezzar scanned the crowd and became enraged to see the three wise men from Judah standing.

"How dare they disobey me!" he cried furiously. "Bring

them to me!"

Once in front of the king, he began to rant and rave.

"Is it true, Shadrach, Meshach and Abednego that you do not serve my gods nor worship the golden image which I have set up?"

"Yes, Nebuchadnezzar, it is true," Shadrach said. Nebuchadnezzar was shocked for he was not even acting afraid.

"And don't you know the consequences of disobeying an edict of the king in this matter?"

"Nebuchadnezzar," Abednego said, "we do know, but..."

"But we cannot bow to anyone but our God," Meshach said.

"He is the One True God," Shadrach said. "And He is able to deliver us out of your hand, O King. But even if He doesn't, we will not serve your gods, nor worship the golden image."

Nebuchadnezzar was furious.

"Heat up the furnace seven times more! You think your God can deliver you? We shall see! Arioch! Send me your mightiest men to bind these three rebels and cast them into the fiery furnace!"

The mighty men came, and threw the three men into the fire. It was so hot that when they threw the captives into the furnace, the mighty men died immediately. But Nebuchadnezzar could not believe his eyes! Not only were the three young men still standing and walking around in the furnace – there was a fourth man standing in the fire with them!

"Weren't only three men thrown into the fire?" Nebuchadnezzar asked.

"Yes, your majesty," the guards replied.

"But there are four men walking around in there! How can that be? My guards were incinerated! And look – the fourth man! He looks . . . he looks . . . he looks like . . . The Son of God. . ."

Nebuchadnezzar could barely speak the last few words. He was filled with awe, and the servants around him could not speak a word. Finally, he swallowed hard and called for the three young men.

"Shadrach! Meshach! Abednego! You are indeed the servants of the Most High God! Come forth! Come hither!"

It was an incredible sight as the three young men emerged from the furnace without even the smell of smoke on their clothes. Nebuchadnezzar knew without a doubt he had seen a miracle.

"Amazing. . ." All the kings, princes, governors, captains and counselors were there to see that fire had no power over these men who served the Lord God.

"Not even a hair of their head was singed!" they cried.

"Their clothes are just the same as they were when they went in!"

"They don't even smell like smoke!"

Nebuchadnezzar, the mighty king who believed that his gods were more powerful than any other, began to worship the One True God.

"Blessed be the God of Shadrach, Meshach and Abednego," he said, "who sent his angel and delivered his servants that trusted in Him! They went against the king's orders and yielded their bodies that they might not serve or worship any god, except their own God!"

"I make a decree!" he shouted. "Every people, nation, and language which speak anything against the God of Shadrach, Meshach and Abednego, shall be cut in pieces, and their houses shall be made a dunghill, because there is no other God that can deliver after this sort!"

"I hereby promote these three men: Shadrach, Meshach and Abednego! They shall be rulers in my kingdom henceforth and forever!"

~~~

Daniel had been summoned again to the king's chambers. Nebuchadnezzar's palace was enormous, and it took Daniel a long time to walk from his rooms by the gate of the city to the king's favorite room. It was cool and comfortable in the thick walls, protected from the harsh sun of the Babylonian desert, and the halls were filled with the sweet scents of jasmine, cinnamon, vanilla, roses and lotus blossoms. There were also the scents of cypress, cedar wood, myrrh and frankincense. The wardrobes of the king and queen were constantly laid out on screens above incense burners so that the scent inundated their clothes and wrapped the nobles in luxurious scent that perfumed the air as they walked past. When they showered (servants poured water over their bodies) they also poured olive oil and perfume over themselves. The nobles of Babylonia oozed fragrance.

Even the temple workers and priests were blessed with the scents in the very pores of their skin after making cubes of incense for the kingdom. They mixed ground gums and plants with honey using ingredients such as calamus, henna, spikenard, frankincense, myrrh, cinnamon, cypress and terebinth. Cedar from Lebanon, as well as pine, fir resin and myrtle were also used. Babylon was a city as delightful to the nose as it was to the eye and people came from afar to buy its perfume.

Daniel continued down the beautifully decorated corridor, where statues of gold, bronze, copper and silver stood upon beautiful rugs and tapestries rich in color, and all made by expert artisans. At the end of the hall, the king's guards opened the thick cedar doors to the king's chamber to let him in. Nebuchadnezzar, his fingers and neck dripping in jewels and gold, was delighted to see Daniel again. He always looked forward to his visits.

"Come in, Daniel, Come in! It is good to see you! I am glad you are here."

"Yes, sire. What is your need?"

"I thought it right to tell you about the signs and wonders that the High God has given me. Oh, how great are His signs, Daniel! How mighty are His wonders! His kingdom is an everlasting kingdom, and His dominion from generation to generation!"

Daniel smiled to himself and looked at the ground. The king had changed much since he saw his friends in the fiery furnace. But he still seemed to think he needed his other gods, too.

"I was resting last night, Daniel, enjoying my palace, just relaxing, when I had a very frightening dream. I brought in all the wise men of Babylon to tell me the interpretation of the dream: all of my magicians, astrologers, and soothsayers, and not one of them could tell me what it means!" The king was pacing the floor, and frantically waving his hands.

"They looked at the entrails of goats and lambs, they have consulted the stars – they can tell me nothing! You must help me, Daniel! This is very troubling and I'm terrified!"

Nebuchadnezzar, the great warrior and mighty king who made all men on earth tremble, was terrified by a dream? Daniel smiled to himself, realizing that God Himself could strike terror in anyone whom He wished.

"As God wills it I will interpret," Daniel nodded. "Go on."

"I saw an enormous tree in the middle of the earth that reached the sky, and everyone on earth could see it," the king said. "Oh, it was a beautiful tree! There was enough fruit on it to feed everyone on earth, and all the animals slept under its shadow. All the birds in the world slept in its boughs."

The king stopped pacing and pondered this a moment. Such a tree it was!

"But then, an angel came down from heaven and shouted, 'Cut down the tree! Shake off the leaves! Scatter the fruit! Scatter the animals and birds! But leave the stump of it in the earth, and let it rain on it seven times, and send the man to live with the beasts of the field until seven times pass over him.'"

Daniel nodded.

"I have the interpretation, Nebuchadnezzar, but you will not like it."

"I don't care!" the king responded in desperation, throwing himself into his chair. "I can't sleep or eat! What good am I anyway? What could be worse? I'm miserable. Tell me! Tell me, Daniel, please!"

"This is the interpretation, O king, and this is the decree of the most High, Who has visited you in your sleep." Daniel paused.

"Well?" the king shouted. "What are you waiting for? Tell me!"

Daniel bravely stood and faced the king.

"They shall drive you from here, and you will eat grass like an ox and will live out of doors where it will rain upon you seven years, until you admit that the most high God rules mankind and gives kingdoms to whomsoever He wills." Daniel turned to look out the open doors onto the balcony of the king's rooms. "After seven years pass, and you admit that it is God Who is in control, you will be restored to your kingdom."

Daniel turned to face the king again, and took his hand as he knelt at his feet. "But, O King, admit this now and avoid this horrible curse! Show mercy to the poor, repent of your sins and live righteously so that you may continue to live in peace and prosperity!"

The king scoffed at Daniel and waved him out of his rooms.

"That is ridiculous," the king said. "Go back to your place, Daniel. I have better things to do than to listen to fantasies."

Daniel left, shaking his head, saddened that the king was too arrogant and vain to listen to God's warnings.

A year after the dream and Daniel's interpretation, Nebuchadnezzar was walking in his palace, boasting.

"Is not this Babylon great, this house of the kingdom that I have built by the might of my power, and for the honor of my majesty?" he said.

But before he could finish his boasting, a voice from heaven spoke to the king:

"O king Nebuchadnezzar, to thee it is spoken; The kingdom is departed from thee. And they shall drive thee from men, and thy dwelling shall be with the beasts of the field: they shall make thee to eat grass as oxen, and seven times shall pass over thee, until thou know that the most High ruleth in the kingdom of men, and giveth it to whomsoever he will." [15]

The king's servants sent for Daniel.

"Quickly, sir, the king – he is acting strangely! We don't know what to do!"

When Daniel arrived, he found the king in his gardens eating grass like an ox.

"It has begun," Daniel said.

"What has begun?" the servant said.

"What God has promised," Daniel said. "Stay with him. Make sure he is cared for. This behavior will last for seven years, so. . ."

"Seven years?" the servant exclaimed. "But what shall I do with him? He refuses to get dressed! He refuses to eat anything but grass!"

"Keep everyone away from him. If people want to see the king, tell them he is not accepting audience. Keep him in the garden. I will check on him regularly."

---

[15] Daniel 4:31,32

As time passed, the king's hair grew as long as an eagle's feathers and his nails grew like a bird's claws. Finally, after seven years of living like a beast, Nebuchadnezzar lifted his eyes up to heaven and began to bless the One True God:

"I bless the most High, and I praise and honor Him that lives for ever, whose dominion is an everlasting dominion, and his kingdom is from generation to generation: And all the inhabitants of the earth are reputed as nothing: and God doeth according to His will in the army of heaven, and among the inhabitants of the earth: and none can stay his hand, or say unto him, What doest thou?"[16]

Immediately, Nebuchadnezzar's madness left him and he became again the honored king of Babylon. He praised, extolled and honored the King of heaven and admitted that God humbles the proud.

Several years later, Nebuchadnezzar went back to Jerusalem again and this time he completely destroyed the temple in Jerusalem and took all the holy vessels to Babylon. He ruled Babylon for 45 years and was about 65 years old when he died.

~~~~~

In 550BC, Belshazzar, the son of Nabonidus, the son of Nebuchadnezzar, became king of Babylonia. One night, in the year 539, he had a party and invited a thousand guests and was using all of the silver and gold vessels from the holy temple in Jerusalem to eat and drink from.

---

[16] See Daniel 4:34,35

"Hail to the god of gold!" he shouted.

"Hail to the god of gold!" the others shouted, laughing, slapping one another on the back, and raising the sacred vessels into the air.

"Hail to the god of silver!" he laughed.

"Hail to the god of silver!" they all yelled, slurping wine.

"Hail to the gods of brass, iron, wood and stone!" he roared, wine dribbling down his chin.

"Hail to the gods of brass, iron, wood and stone!" they all shouted, pouring wine down their throats and laughing uproariously.

Suddenly, Belshazzar turned pale and dropped his glass. People choked and the women screamed and hid behind the men. Wine spilled everywhere in the room and it became deathly quiet.

"Wh-wh-what is THAT?" someone whispered, pointing to the wall.

The king was terrified and shaking. In front of him was a giant hand writing words on the wall: "MENE, MENE, TEKEL, UPHARSIN."

"G-g-g-go g-g-get th-the w-wise m-m-men," the king croaked. The servants scattered and went to gather every sage of the kingdom for the king. When they returned, the king was wringing his hands and sweating.

"Whoever can read this writing, and show me the interpretation, shall be clothed with scarlet, and given a chain of gold to wear about his neck, and shall be the third ruler in the kingdom!" he blurted.

The king tried to act bold and brave, but everyone could

see that his knees were knocking under his garments. The wise men all shrugged and looked at one another. They were in awe – they had never seen such a thing -- but none of them could tell the king what it meant.

"Out! Out with the lot of you! What good are you to me if you can't even answer my questions?" The king was downcast and sullen.

The Queen had not been invited to the party, but heard about the handwriting on the wall, and came to see what was taking place there. She found the king perplexed and went to comfort him.

"Do not worry so, King," she said. "There is a man in the kingdom, in whom is the spirit of the holy gods; and in the days of the kings before you, light and understanding and wisdom, like the wisdom of the gods, was found in him. Nebuchadnezzar made him master of the magicians, astrologers, Chaldeans, and soothsayers."

King Belshazzar raised his eyebrows and listened to his queen. He remembered hearing his grandfather tell stories about Daniel.

"This same man has an excellent spirit, and knowledge, and understanding," the queen said soothingly. "He is able to interpret dreams, and read difficult language. He will show you the interpretation, I am certain," she murmured to the king, who was calmer now.

"Bring him," he said.

Daniel was brought before the king. He looked at the holy vessels strewn about the room and then at the writing on the wall, and then at the king.

"Is your name Daniel?" the king asked. "The one who was brought here a captive from Judah?"

"Yes," Daniel replied.

"I have heard that the spirit of God is in you, and that light and understanding and excellent wisdom is found in you." The king paused and looked Daniel over carefully, and then pointed to the wall.

"The wise men and astrologers were brought in before me to read this writing and interpret it for me, but they could not. If you can read the writing, and tell me what it means, you will be clothed with scarlet, and have a chain of gold to wear around your neck, and you will be the third ruler in the kingdom."

"I don't want your gifts," Daniel answered. "Give them to someone else. I will read the writing and tell you what it means." Daniel looked around him again at the holy vessels scattered about the floor and then up at the king.

"The most high God gave your forefather, Nebuchadnezzar, a kingdom with majesty and glory and honor. The whole world feared him and trembled. But he became proud, so God allowed his heart to become like a beast's, and his dwelling was with the wild animals. He ate grass like oxen, and his body was wet with the dew of heaven until he realized that the most high God ruled in the kingdom of men, and that He makes king over it whomsoever He will. And you, His descendant, O Belshazzar, have not humbled your heart, even though you knew all of this." Daniel shook his head in disappointment.

"You have lifted yourself up against the Lord of heaven and allowed vessels of God's house to be brought before you.

You and your nobles, wives, and concubines, have drunk wine in them and have praised the gods of silver, and gold, of brass, iron, wood, and stone, which do not see or hear or know you or anything else. And God - who holds your breath in his hand, and in whose hand are all your ways – you have not glorified. That is why He sent that hand to write."

Daniel walked to the wall and looked at it.

"This is the interpretation," Daniel said, turning boldly to the king. "'Mene:' God has numbered the days of your kingdom and finished it. 'Tekel:' You are weighed in the balances and found wanting. 'Peres:' Your kingdom will be divided and given to the Medes and Persians."

Ironically, Belshazzar was thrilled to know the meaning. Perhaps he didn't really believe it, or perhaps he was just too drunk to understand.

"I command that Daniel be clothed in scarlet and a chain of gold put around his neck. I hereby make him the third ruler of the kingdom!" the king shouted, and celebrated that he knew the meaning of the handwriting on the wall.

But that night, Belshazzar was killed, just as the hand had written, and Darius, the Mede, took the kingdom at the age of 62.

~~~~~

Darius the Mede placed 120 princes over his kingdom, and over the princes he set three presidents, and Daniel was the first over all of them.

Darius loved Daniel. He enjoyed his company, and had a lot of respect for his work because an excellent spirit was in him. But this made the presidents and princes jealous, and they constantly tried to find fault with him or catch him in mistakes. But Daniel was a man of integrity, and they could never catch him doing anything wrong.

"We'll never find anything against this Daniel," they complained. "We need a plan." And they began to scheme how they could get Daniel into trouble.

One day these influencial men approached the king with a plan they had designed that would eliminate Daniel from the kingdom.

"King Darius, live forever," they said. "We have been consulting regarding a matter. Cause a royal statue to be established and make a firm decree that if anyone prays to any other god except you and your statue, they shall be cast into a den of lions."

King Darius, like other kings before him, was vain enough to think this was a great idea. He signed the law, and once a king had signed a decree, it could not be taken back.

When Daniel heard about this law, he didn't change any of his praying habits. He still went into his house three times a day, knelt and gave a prayer of thanks in his window facing Jerusalem, as he had always done.

This was exactly what the other rulers wanted Daniel to do, and they went to the king and said, "Didn't you sign a decree that anyone who prays to another god besides you shall be cast into the den of lions? O King, Daniel is not praying to you. He goes to his window to pray three times a day to his own God."

When the king heard their words, he was sorry he had ever signed such a decree, and he worked until sundown trying to find a way around the law. But it was impossible. According to the law of the Medes and Persians, no decree or statute that the king established could be reversed.

The king had no choice but to command the guards to cast Daniel into the den of lions.

"Daniel!" he called into the den. "The God that you serve continually – He will deliver you!"

The guards laid a large stone upon the mouth of the den, and the king sealed it with his own signet and the signet of the lords. Then, he went into his palace and stayed up all night fasting for the safety of Daniel.

When morning came, the king quickly went to the mouth of the den and cried sadly to Daniel. "Daniel! O Daniel, servant of the Living God – is your God, the One you serve continually, able to deliver you from the lions?"

Before the king could hear the echo of his own words, he heard Daniel answer him. "O King! My God sent His angel and shut the lions' mouths and they haven't harmed me because I was found innocent in His eyes!"

Darius felt deep joy when he heard Daniel's voice, and he commanded that Daniel be taken up out of the den at once. "You don't even have a scratch on you, Daniel!" the king said, embracing him. "And now," he said, "bring those men that accused Daniel and cast *them* into this den of lions!"

King Darius went back to his palace and wrote to all people on earth:

"Peace be multiplied unto you. I make a decree, That in every dominion of my kingdom men tremble and fear before the God of

Daniel: for he is the living God, and steadfast forever, and his kingdom that which shall not be destroyed, and his dominion shall be even unto the end. He delivereth and rescueth, and he worketh signs and wonders in heaven and in earth, who hath delivered Daniel from the power of the lions."[17]

Epilogue

Daniel prospered in the reign of Darius, and in the reign of Cyrus the Persian after him. God had even more for Daniel to do. He gave Daniel many prophetic dreams about the future, which continue to be read and studied and debated today. Many of his dreams are mysterious and include images of beasts and wars. Daniel himself could not discern their meanings.

"But Lord," he asked, "What is the meaning of these dreams I have written? O my Lord, what shall be the end of these things?"

But God would not tell him. Instead He said, "Go thy way, Daniel: for the words are closed up and sealed till the time of the end. Many shall be purified, and made white, and tried; but the wicked shall do wickedly: and none of the wicked shall understand; but the wise shall understand..."[18]

Ironically, Daniel, the man who always gave God the glory for giving him the interpretations of the king's dreams,

---

[17] Daniel 6:25-27
[18] Daniel 12:9-12

died not understanding or knowing the meaning of his own dreams and visions. Their meanings and interpretations are yet to be fully revealed.

About the Author

Karla Akins is married to her pastor-husband, Eddie (Edward); and is mother (and mother-in-love) to Melissa and her husband Brent; Jesse and his wife, Kara; Noah, 15; and Isaiah and Isaac, 11. She has three granddaughters, Abigail, Lauren and Trinity. Her favorite food is ice cream and her new hobby is riding  her motorcycle and taking pictures of rural Indiana. Karla has homeschooled for more than 18 years. She continues to homeschool her three youngest boys and other students at her cottage school in the town of North Manchester where she resides with her family and a funny little pug, an elderly dachshund and a friendly, loving rottweiler.

To Nathan and Peter

He has told you, O man, what is good;
and what does the LORD require of you
but to do justice, and to love kindness,
and to walk humbly with your God?

Micah 6:8 (ESV)

Cyrus the Great
Mighty Warrior, Gentle King

by Kathleen Jacobs

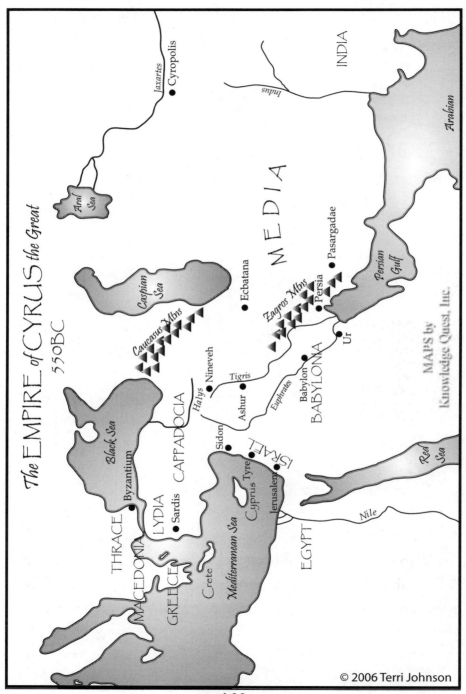

The EMPIRE of CYRUS the Great
550 BC

MAPS by
Knowledge Quest, Inc.

© 2006 Terri Johnson

6

Cyrus the Great
Mighty Warrior, Gentle King

by Kathleen Jacobs

early 2500 years ago, in a broad valley ringed by mighty mountains, a newborn boy tested his voice with strong, demanding cries. Well might he cry, for a harsh and dangerous world greeted him! In the months before his birth, baby Cyrus had already gained a powerful enemy: Astyages, king of the Median Empire.

From his throne in northwestern Iran, Astyages controlled territories stretching from modern Afghanistan to Turkey. Astyages jealously guarded his throne, suspicious of any who might attempt to overthrow him. Disturbing dreams had troubled his sleep and agitated his waking moments. Years before, he had dreamt of a flood that raged through his city, breeching the walls with its swirling fury and surging until its churning waters covered Asia. King Astyages had concluded that his kingdom must be in danger. His downfall must be at hand! To protect against the danger of a strong, ambitious son-in-law or grandson, he married his daughter Mandane to Cambyses, the weak king of Persia. Certainly, he calculated, this semi-nomadic region located just north of the Persian Gulf would never produce a ruler who would rise against him.

But another dream had come, haunting his sleep with a vision of a vigorous vine snaking through the streets, stretching its tendrils to cover the farthest reaches of Asia. Once again, Astyages had awoken with the fear that his empire and throne were in danger. Driven by these fears, the king had consulted the magi. Surely his wise advisors could explain the meaning of these nightmares and devise a way to avoid disaster.

The magi's eyes had darkened as they listened. "A baby will be born to your daughter, Mandane," one had explained. "When this child grows into strong manhood, he will challenge your power, Great King."

But if the baby never reached manhood…

Kind Astyages had quickly sent messengers to Perisa to bring Mandane home to the royal court in the city of Ecbatana. Although she was expecting the birth of a child, Mandane had endured the uncomfortable, winding journey through the Zagros Mountains to Ecbatana where her father anxiously waited.

King Astyages had determined he must end the threat to his throne. With Mandane safely within his palace walls, he had restlessly waited for the birth of her child. As soon as Cyrus entered the world, Astyages summoned a trusted official named Harpagus and whispered chilling orders: "You must seize Mandane's child, carry him to your home, and slay him!"

The kidnapping was quickly accomplished. Only when baby Cyrus was hidden within his home, did Harpagus pause to consider the task before him. Although he had certainly seen the horrors of battle and even killed men, he found he could not raise his hand against this baby. Instead, he summoned a herdsman named Mitradates. Handing him the tiny bundle, Harpagus whispered instructions: "The king commands that you carry this child far into the desolate mountains. There, you must abandon him in the wilderness."

Mitradates secretly set out with the child. His thoughts raced ahead to his simple home where his wife was mourning the death of their newborn child. He walked quickly through the village and darted into his own house. "Look!" he whispered to his pale, bedridden wife as he pulled back the splendid clothes that swaddled the child and quickly told her the errand he had been given

His wife gazed in amazement at the cooing, squirming bundle. Her own precious baby, whom she had cradled that very morning, had been cold and silent, having met death before birth; but this boy was brimming with warm life. Though she had already shed many tears for her own son, the weary woman now wept for the doomed child before her. "Do not let him die," she pleaded. "Our own son was stillborn. This child shall be our son from this day forward. You must leave our own dead child on the mountain in his place!"

Hearing her words, Mitradates' heart strengthened with resolve: he would not be a partner with those who sought this baby's death. Though he had been unable to prevent the death of his own son, he would save this child! Quickly pulling the royal robes from Cyrus, he dressed the dead child in the finery. Mitradates then slipped from the house and began to climb, following paths that led to the remote pastures crowned by barren mountain peaks. There would be a lone baby on the mountain that night, but that little one no longer possessed a life that could be threatened by the cruelties of nature.

~~~~~

Cyrus grew strong and tall in the herdsman's home. When he was ten years old, his playmates insisted that he must play the part of the king in their game. He performed admirably, assigning work and positions of rank to different boys. One lad refused to cooperate, and Cyrus ordered a whipping for the offender who happened to be the son of an important Mede. The boy was shocked to receive such treatment from a herdsman's son and determined that his father should hear of this outrage.

News of this event eventually reached Astyages, and he summoned the boy who had treated the son of his noble so rudely. Cyrus answered the king's questions with straightforward wisdom. Suddenly Astyages guessed the truth. Such a valiant and strong child must have royal parents. His grandson must have survived the cruel sentence placed on him at birth.

Astyages was so pleased with his grandson that he abandoned plans for his death and returned him to his parents in Persia. Towards Harpagus, the noble who had obediently kidnapped baby Cyrus, however, he was not so kind. The disobedient subject was forced to endure terrible punishment, which he never forgot.

~~~~~

Thus ends the dramatic story of Cyrus's birth, which has been retold for generations. The legend became famous when a Greek historian named Herodotus included it in *The History of Herodotus*, a famous Greek classic that earned him the title, "Father of History." This story along with many tales of intrigue and military triumph had been told to Herdotus as he traveled in the Persian Empire less than one hundred years after Cyrus' death.

Herodotus also heard other versions of Cyrus' birth, including one involving a wolf mother who nursed the abandoned baby Cyrus when he lay alone in the field.

Any portrait of Cyrus the Great consists of a skeleton of facts surrounded by the flesh of legend, controversy, and imaginative guesswork. The resulting image is larger than life. Those who study the life of Cyrus must decide — among other things — which stories are believable, what archaeological artifacts belong to his reign, and how particular manuscripts should be dated. The answers to such questions will dictate the picture of Cyrus and of Persian history that emerges.

~~~~~

The study of ancient history at the time of Cyrus' birth tends to focus on the four great powers which dominated the territories stretching from the Mediterranean Sea eastward to the foothills of the majestic Himalayas: Media, Babylon, Lydia, and Egypt. There was a delicate balance of power among these four, which was frighteningly disrupted when Cyrus, the son of a weak Persian king, reached manhood and began to fight. Before his first battle, the world had hardly noticed the loosely united Persian tribes that inhabited the harsh plains of the Iranian plateau. This changed as Cyrus emerged from his tiny kingdom to startle the world with his mighty rise to power. For over two hundred years his family of Persian kings, known today as the Achaemenid Dynasty, would rule the vast empire he founded.

When Cyrus began to reign sometime around 559 B.C, his kingdom covered a small section of Iranian territory north of the Persian Gulf. He could not claim this humble region entirely as his own, for his grandfather, Astyages, reigned as overlord of all parts of the Median Empire, including Persia. Neither Cyrus nor his Persian followers appreciated this foreign control. Soon, Cyrus began planning a revolt against his grandfather. According to Herodotus, the young Persian ruler was encouraged in these efforts by the injured and revengeful Harpagus.[1]

No one is exactly sure how the war between Media and Persia began, but the end is undisputed. Cyrus seized the victory and gained control of all Median territories. These included much of the old Assyrian Empire, and a strategic position along the east-west trade route.

Astyages lost his empire, but Cyrus mercifully spared his grandfather's life and allowed him to retain his noble lifestyle. Other Median nobles were granted positions of honor in Cyrus' government, and his empire is sometimes called the Medo-Persian Empire. Harpagus, who assisted Cyrus by betraying King Astyages during battle, earned a position in Cyrus' army

---

[1] Herodotus. *The History of Herodotus* 1.123 Rawlinson

as one of his most trusted and successful generals.

News of Cyrus' victory over Media spread through the Near East. Now that one of the four great powers had tumbled, the others felt a tremor they feared might herald a coming earthquake that would topple their own strongholds. Would Cyrus be content to rule within the borders of the Medo-Persian Empire? Or would messengers soon bring news of a mighty Persian army descending from the Iranian mountains to challenge the ancient powers on the Mesopotamian plain below? Surely the rulers of the day searched for some clue of his ambitions just as historians today continue to sift through ancient archives for evidence of whether Cyrus, the young ruler of tiny Persia, dreamed of commanding a vast empire. The leaders of Egypt, Babylonia, and Lydia (in modern Turkey) took no chances. They formed an alliance to protect against the new force rising in the east.

Sometime around 547 to 545 B.C., Lydia's famously wealthy King Croesus[2] decided to move against Cyrus. According to Herodotus, the Lydian king guessed that it might take some time for Cyrus to fully organize his government and strengthen his army after the victory over Media. Croesus hoped to move quickly and catch Cyrus unprepared.[3]

Before marching to battle, however, Croesus wanted to be certain of victory. He would courageously command the first rush of Lydian horses into the Persian army's lines if he knew

---

[2] "Rich as Croesus" is an idiom used today to indicate that someone possesses extreme wealth.
[3] Herodotus 1.46

the battle would end with Lydia's victory. If only he could glimpse the future! All he needed was a dependable prophet.

Nearby Greece had a plentiful supply of such prophets, known as oracles, who lived in temples in various cities. Croesus determined that the temple at Delphi housed the most trustworthy oracle. Eager for guidance, the Lydian king loaded his messengers with gifts and commanded them to ask the Delphi oracle whether he should march against Cyrus. The oracle assured Croesus that if he attacked the Persians, he would destroy a mighty empire. Croesus rejoiced! Victory waited only on his action against Cyrus.

Confidently, Croesus crossed the river Halys[4] which had long formed the boundary between Lydia in the west and Media and Persia in the east. As he marched through Cappadocia in modern Turkey, he destroyed the countryside and asserted himself as the ruler of cities that had long been under Median rule. This was an offense against Cyrus, the new ruler of all the old Median lands.

Cyrus would not allow his empire to be snatched from his grasp. Without delay, he marched to challenge Croesus. While it is possible that he started from Iran, it is also possible that Cyrus was already campaigning in the eastern regions of Cappadocia, strengthening his control over former Median territories. A grueling distance of well over 1000 miles lay between Iran and Cappadocia, a march of over two months. No one knows exactly where Cyrus first heard the news

---

[4] Today this river is known as the **Kizil Irmak**. It flows through Turkey.

that Croesus meant to attack him, but at some point Cyrus successfully moved his army across the impressive distance between Iran and the Lydian army.

Such a feat required superb organization. Daily nuisances such as ill soldiers, stuck wagons, and narrow mountain passes required attention. Skilled workers were needed to shoe horses and repair chariots. Most importantly, even in the driest terrain, the commander must provide water and food. Hunger and thirst could quickly destroy the mightiest army. Despite these challenges, Cyrus repeatedly proved himself an effective military campaigner. During the long march, the Persian army actually strengthened as it advanced. Along the route, Cyrus gathered new recruits, forging an army that would be ready to stand against Croesus.

The meeting of the two armies in November erupted into a bloody battle that lasted until nightfall. Despite the intense fighting, neither army could claim victory. When Cyrus did not attack the next day, Croesus decided to head for home, confident that Cyrus would not follow. Winter approached, the season when armies sought the safety of home before the brutal, frigid storms invaded. Winter would provide Croesus the time he needed to recruit support from Sparta, Babylon, and Egypt for a mighty spring offensive against Cyrus.

Safely back home in his capital city of Sardis, Croesus sent some soldiers home for the winter. He also began drafting requests for aid from his allies. Imagine his surprise when a jagged line of javelins gleamed tauntingly on the far side of the broad, barren plain that spread beneath the citadel of Sardis. In daring defiance of the oncoming winter, Cyrus had decided

175

to advance on Sardis at once rather than face overwhelming enemy forces in the spring. Croesus decided to ride out of the city to meet Cyrus in battle.

Cyrus had already made shrewd preparations. He had determined that the spears of Lydia's renowned cavalry posed a great threat to his soldiers. He prepared a unique defense. Cyrus ordered his men to remove the luggage from the pack camels. The gaunt beasts were granted a nobler task on that day than any they had ever known, for in the hour of battle, they would carry the king's mighty warriors in the attack.

Urging their strange mounts forward, the Persians advanced to meet the long lances of the mighty Lydian cavalry. Reacting as though guided by Cyrus's hand, the Lydian horses bucked and retreated, spooked by the Persian camels; for as Herodotus noted, horses cannot stand the smell of camels.[5] The Lydian warriors jumped to the ground and continued the fight on foot, but after horrible loss on both sides, Croesus retreated within the walls of Sardis. The Persians besieged the city.

People in that day believed that the Sardis walls could not be breeched. A portion of the wall even crowned a high cliff. Only a long siege could force the citadel to surrender. Cyrus, however, was not content to wait endless months while the citizens of Sardis supped on their vast stores of food. He would attack. But first, Cyrus announced that a prize awaited the first man who managed to mount the walls. Eager for this prize, his soldiers advanced, only to be successfully repelled by the Lydians.

---

[5] Herodotus 1.80

In the end, Sardis met defeat through a simple careless act by a single Lydian soldier. When this man's helmet dropped over the wall and rolled down the steep cliff, he hurried after it. He carefully descended the cliff by a familiar path. Grasping the stray helmet, he retraced his steps and hastily returned to his post. Little did he guess that the price of his lost helmet would be the kingdom of Lydia.

On the plain below, a Persian soldier had carefully observed the Lydian's path up the cliff. As the section of wall above the "insurmountable" cliff was lazily guarded, he easily led a group of Persian soldiers to the top. They entered the city, threw open the gates, and Cyrus' army poured victoriously into Sardis! An empire had fallen just as Croesus had been told by the oracle, but it was Lydia, not Persia, that suffered defeat.

Since Cyrus had a growing empire to manage and other lands to conquer, he left Lydia under the rule of Tabalus, a Persian. This man's official position was that of satrap, which meant he governed a specific region of the Persian Empire (called a satrapy). A satrap's job was to function as Cyrus' representative, doing exactly what his leader would have desired. He often worked with local officials who had served the previous, conquered ruler. This system of administration allowed Cyrus effectively to govern an empire larger than any the world had yet seen.

Satraps faced many challenges, as Tabalus discovered. Some of the local officials in Lydia proved treacherous and stirred up a revolt against the Persian leadership. Cyrus responded with swift severity. At his command, another Median general, Mazares, raced back to Sardis and squashed the rebellion. Soon after, Harpagus the Mede became the satrap of Sardis. He continued to prove his worthiness by conquering Ionia on the edge of the Aegean Sea for Cyrus.

Each Persian victory increased Cyrus's wealth. With the defeat of Sardis, Cyrus not only gained control of Lydian territories, but he also became owner of the vast Lydian treasury which he sent back to Ecbatana to help finance his campaigns. Perhaps more importantly, the conquest added soldiers to Cyrus's army and supplied skilled craftsmen for his projects.

~~~~~

In addition to his conquests, Cyrus also devoted attention to building projects. Lydian and Ionian stonemasons had a strong influence on the construction and decoration of a capital city that Cyrus built in his Iranian homeland. There, on a high, fertile plain ringed by mountains, they constructed the royal city of Pasargadae.

The design of the beautiful palaces and halls displayed the influence of many cultures and testified to the use of foreign craftsmen. Splendid limestone columns and detailed reliefs decorated the buildings and displayed the might and luxury of the Persian court.

The same beautiful design extended outdoors. Cyrus and the Persian kings who followed him loved gardens. In fact, the English word paradise comes from the Persian word for a garden park. At Parsargadae the king's throne was placed so that he might gaze upon the orderly gardens that surrounded the palace. Lush garden beds were artfully bordered by stone-lined irrigation canals that supplied the dry, but fertile soil with precious water.

Today in Parsargadae, silent sentinels haunt a peaceful landscape. Broken stone columns jut skyward like the stump remains of a once-mighty forest. The canals are dry, the gardens erased by a brushy carpet of tall grasses and scarlet poppies that once again controls the land.

~~~~~

In the mid-sixth century, Cyrus was the undisputed ruler of Pasargadae and his empire was expanding. With the capture of Sardis, Cyrus completed his conquest of two of the four great kingdoms that had ruled the world of his birth. Media and Lydia were under his control; Babylon and Egypt remained. Both warily watched this giant from the east.

Although the precise timeline of Cyrus' campaigns is unknown, it is likely that soon after the conquest of Lydia, he marched northeast beyond the Iranian salt desert. There, in territory rich with lapis-lazuli mines, he conquered lands beyond the Oxus River[6] at least as far as the Jaxartes River.[7]

The Central Asian tribes possessed fierce warriors who disrupted the peace along the northern and eastern borders of the Persian Empire. To protect his territory from such vicious attacks, Cyrus built several defense forts along the Jaxartes River. When his eastern border was secured and his army strengthened by soldiers from his newly acquired territories, Cyrus once again turned his attention west to his next great opponent, Babylon.

---

[6] Today this river is known as the Amu Darya. It forms the northern border of Afghanistan.
[7] Today this river is known as the Syr Darya. It flows through Tajikistan, Uzbekistan, and Kazakhstan.

The Babylonian territory stretched between the Tigris and Euphrates Rivers. For years, this mighty kingdom had dominated the region, expanding by destroying smaller kingdoms. The Old Testament gives a detailed account of the experience of the kingdom of Judah at the hands of the Babylonians.

In 722 B.C. Assyria destroyed the Northern Kingdom of Israel. The people in the Southern Kingdom of Judah were left with fears that they would soon suffer the same fate as their northern brothers. Their fearful gaze flittered between the might of Assyria, which had overthrown Israel, and the strengthening Babylon, which had begun to threaten even mighty Assyria.

The prophet Isaiah criticized Judah's attempts to form alliances with other countries. The kingdom of Judah must trust in their God, Yahweh, alone for protection. Driven by fear, the leaders of Judah refused to listen to his warning, and continued to seek protective military alliances. Isaiah declared that the result would be destruction for the kingdom of Judah: "Behold, the days are coming when all that is in your house, and that which your fathers have stored up till this day, shall be carried to Babylon. Nothing shall be left says the Lord" (Isaiah 39:6 ESV). But Isaiah followed this declaration with words of comfort: Yahweh would not abandon his people in Babylon; he would send a savior to rescue them:

"I stirred up one from the north, and he has come,
from the rising of the sun, and he shall call upon my name;
he shall trample on rulers as on mortar,
as the potter treads clay." (Isaiah 41:25 ESV)

181

In 586 B.C,. however, no savior arose to protect Judah, and Isaiah's predicted destruction fell upon the kingdom. The final paragraphs of II Chronicles describe the devastating details:

"And they burned the house of God and broke down the wall of Jerusalem and burned all its palaces with fire and destroyed all its precious vessels. He (the Babylonian king) took into exile in Babylon those who had escaped from the sword, and they became servants to him and to his sons until the establishment of the kingdom of Persia...seventy years [later]." (II Chronicles 36:19-20, 21b ESV)

Seventy years! The captives faced a long wait for the predicted savior who Isaiah claimed would overthrow Babylon and release them from captivity. Only the youngest exiles would live to see him enter the city gates.

It is interesting to imagine the captives recalling Isaiah's predictions, possibly even reading copies of his words as they suffered in Babylon. Did they whisper the prophecies in the dead of night and wonder about their meaning? Did they cling to hope, trusting that Yahweh would fulfill his promises? The prophesied destruction had come; would the predicted savior follow? Imagine their amazement when they first heard the news that a new warrior, one named Cyrus, had conqueror the Medes and the Lydians. Surely, Isaiah's words then echoed in their minds:

*"Thus says the LORD to his anointed, to Cyrus,
whose right hand I have grasped,
to subdue nations before him
and to loose the belts of kings,*

to open doors before him
that gates may not be closed."
(Isaiah 45:1 ESV)

This passage is remarkable in many ways. The Old Testament focused on God's work among the people of Israel. It is rare for a non-Jewish person to be discussed and even rarer for that person to be praised. Yet Cyrus is given the title of honor, "The Lord's Anointed," even though God says, "...you do not acknowledge me" (Isaiah 45:4). God chose Cyrus for a specific, great act of salvation; and through Isaiah, God announced Cyrus' coming and his name years before his birth.

~~~~~

By 539 B.C., Cyrus certainly had heard reports that all was not well in Babylon. The king, Nabonidus, had moved to Arabia — hundreds of miles away from his capital — and had left the city in the hands of his unpopular son, King Belshazzar, who ruled as his co-regent. Nabonidus had also shown a preference for the moon god Sin rather than the traditionally popular god Marduk. This had angered many Babylonians, who believed that their own well-being depended on the king keeping the gods happy. Cyrus may have organized covert missions within Babylon aimed at watering this discontent and sowing seeds that would bloom into a joyful welcome when he rode victoriously into Babylon.

Cyrus entered Babylonian territory from the north with a great force. On a small, barrel-shaped clay cylinder, known today as the Cyrus Cylinder, he described his vast army: "...their number, like that of the water of a river, could not be

183

established...."[8] At the city of Opis on the Tigris River, Cyrus defeated the Babylonian army, which retreated and withdrew behind the thick walls of the city of Babylon. The Persian troops followed.

With thick walls and vast stores of provisions, Babylon was well prepared to endure a siege. Even with the Persians at his gates, King Belshazzar hosted a great banquet within the safe, luxurious core of the city.

Meanwhile, Cyrus devised a daring plan. The Tigris River divided the mighty city in two. On each side of the river, tall, thick walls protected each half while holding the water's flow to a straight course. A bridge joined two mighty gates, one in each of the river walls. Cyrus determined that this watery corridor was the key to victory. He placed some of his troops upstream with shovels and ordered the others to gather along the river both above and below the city. The first group dug a channel to a nearby basin, redirecting the waters and dramatically reducing the flow of the river. As soon as the soldiers stationed downriver perceived that the water had vanished, they rushed down the banks, flooding the soggy riverbed with men. Silently, Persian troops flowed in the place of water, their advance unnoticed by the citizens who were absorbed in a loud festival celebration. The Persians entered the city through the open river gates, and the mighty city of Babylon fell without a fight.

Still, the feast of King Belshazzar continued. News of the defeat had not penetrated through the palace walls. Suddenly,

---

[8]*Cyrus Cylinder, (Ancient Near Eastern Texts Relating to the Old Testament,* translated by A. Leo Oppenheim)

a mysterious event silenced all mirth. In clear view, "...the fingers of a human hand appeared and wrote on the plaster of the wall..." (Daniel 5:5). The king and his guests trembled in fear at this haunting sight! No one understood the words: "Mene, Mene, Tekel, Parsin" (Daniel 5:25).

"Call for the wise men!" the nobles cried, but none of the Babylonian magi could explain the writing on the wall. Finally, the queen suggested they summon a Hebrew named Daniel who had served as an advisor to Babylonian rulers since being brought to the city as a captive seventy years earlier.

When Daniel arrived, he interpreted the words as God's declaration that Belshazzar's kingdom was at an end and would be handed to the Medes and the Persians. Daniel 5:30 records the event that soon followed: "That very night Belshazzar...was killed" (*ESV*).

~~~~~

On October 29, 539 B.C., Cyrus the conqueror paraded into Babylon. The people carpeted the road before him with green branches. In the Cyrus Cylinder, Cyrus himself described the warm welcome he received from the people of the city of Babylon, "All the inhabitants of Babylon...bowed to him and kissed his feet, jubilant that he (had received) the kingship..... Happily they greeted him as a master through whose help they had come (again) to life from death..."[9] Written declarations like these display both Cyrus' desire to craft a peaceful transfer of power, and his artful use of propaganda to sway the citizens' emotions towards his rule.

---

[9] *Cyrus Cylinder*, (*Ancient Near Eastern Texts Relating to the Old Testament*, translated by A. Leo Oppenheim)

The Cyrus Cylinder allows the modern world to eavesdrop as Cyrus the Great, newly-crowned king of Babylon, declared his might: "I am Cyrus, king of the world, great king, legitimate king, king of Babylon, king of Sumer and Akkad, king of the four rims (of the earth)..."[10] Yet in his bold praise of himself, Cyrus often displayed an interesting blend of arrogance and benevolence that stands out as remarkable for an ancient ruler. He boasts of kindness rather than cruel conquest: "My numerous troops walked around in Babylon in peace, I did not allow anybody to terrorize...."[11] He notes that he improved bad housing in the city, and restored the foreign idols that Babylon had plundered years before to their temples. He also allowed captive peoples to return to their homes. The record of these actions has earned praise from modern scholars who have declared the Cyrus Cylinder to be an early charter of human rights.

Cyrus' policies impacted the captive Jews who longed to return home to Judah. The promised savior had come to rescue them from exile! Both the final words of II Chronicles and the opening chapter of Ezra record Cyrus's actions:

"In the first year of Cyrus king of Persia, that the word of the LORD by the mouth of Jeremiah might be fulfilled, the LORD stirred up the spirit of Cyrus king of Persia, so that he made a proclamation throughout all his kingdom and also put it in writing: 'Thus says Cyrus king of Persia: The LORD, the God of heaven, has given me

[10] *Cyrus Cylinder*, (*Ancient Near Eastern Texts Relating to the Old Testament*, translated by A. Leo Oppenheim)
[11] *Cyrus Cylinder*, (*Ancient Near Eastern Texts Relating to the Old Testament*, translated by A. Leo Oppenheim)

all the kingdoms of the earth, and he has charged me to build him a house at Jerusalem, which is in Judah. Whoever is among you of all his people, may his God be with him, and let him go up to Jerusalem, which is in Judah and rebuild the house of the LORD, the God of Israel--he is the God who is in Jerusalem." (Ezra 1:1-4 ESV)

Cyrus also ordered that the gold and silver vessels that Nebuchadnezzar had taken from the temple should be returned.

~~~~~

After his first year as ruler in Babylon, Cyrus returned to Ecbatana. Despite the fact that he traveled an amazing number of miles and conquered more territory than any ruler before him, he did not spend all his time on rigorous military campaigns. At times he did return home to the mountain-ringed plains of Iran, pausing for a season in palaces that had long waited for their king. He also moved between different cities in his empire, choosing the mountains during the sizzling hot summers and reaching the warmer climates before biting wind and deathly cold invaded the mountain cities. These palace periods were times for managing his government, enforcing his plans for the empire, and enjoying elaborate feasts and fabled royal hunts. Even the excitement of a lion hunt, however, could not keep Cyrus peacefully homebound. Before long, the call to conquest always lured him away to new adventures on strange frontiers.

Sometime around 530 B.C., an aging Cyrus mustered his army for a campaign in the north. Central Asian tribes in the area near the Aral Sea were raiding the border of his empire. One of those tribes, the Massagetae, was ruled by a queen named Tomyris. Under her command, the Massagetae warriors confronted the Persians in a brutal battle. Cyrus' army suffered terrible losses, including a mortal wound to their mighty king.

The Persian soldiers carried their fallen leader's body back to Pasargadae where a stone tomb awaited. A golden coffin lay within, and other valuable items filled the tomb: a fabulous carpet, tunics and royal robes, jewelry, and weapons. Such a treasure must be protected, and a building stood nearby to house magi who would guard the tomb and offer sacrifices for Cyrus.

Before his death, Cyrus had decreed that his son Cambyses II should succeed him as ruler of the Persian Empire. Cambyses further enlarged the empire by accomplishing Cyrus' goal of conquering Egypt. The government structure that Cyrus had created and executed successfully held the empire together following his death.

~~~~~

Cyrus the Great holds a unique position of honor in history. Even the descendants of his enemies, men like the Greek historian Herodotus, admired Cyrus for his military brilliance and his wise and benevolent governing style. Another Greek, Xenophon, wrote an account of Cyrus which romanticized his life and sought to teach honorable conduct using the example of Cyrus. Even the Macedonian, Alexander the Great, who destroyed the Persian Empire in the fourth century B.C., respected Cyrus. When Alexander marched victoriously through Iran in 324 B.C., two hundred years after Cyrus' death, he paused at the royal park at Pasargadae. His purpose was to pay homage to the founder of the empire he now destroyed.

A thick grove of exotic trees and a meadow watered by streams surrounded the stone tomb of Cyrus the Great. Layers of steep steps, each the height of a soldier, gradually rose in the form of a low ziggurat topped by a simple stone mausoleum. Squeezing through the narrow door, Alexander found that the tomb had been robbed and vandalized. Most of the treasure was missing, including a famous cloak that had belonged to Cyrus. Every Persian emperor had donned this robe as a part of his coronation ceremony, but such an honor would not mark Alexander's claim to Persia. Instead, Alexander, the next ruler that history would title "Great" would honor Cyrus. The Macedonian ordered the restoration and maintenance of Cyrus the Great's tomb, paying tribute to the ruler who had wielded a mighty sword, yet worn a gentle crown.

About the Author

Kathleen L. Jacobs is a writer and homeschooling mother. She lives in Charlotte, North Carolina with her husband and four children. She particularly delights in sharing her love of history and writing with her family. Her first historical novel, *Never Forsaken* (Crossway), tells the story of a German immigrant family. She also contributed a biography about Martin Luther to an earlier volume in this series, *What Really Happened During the Middle Ages.*

For Scott

Eratosthenes
A Friend of Learning

by Susannah Rice

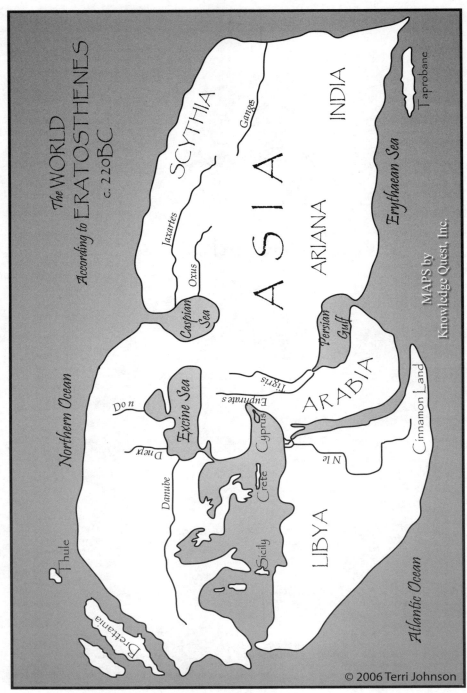

The WORLD
According to ERATOSTHENES
c. 220BC

MAPS by
Knowledge Quest, Inc.

© 2006 Terri Johnson

7

Eratosthenes
A Friend of Learning

by Susannah Rice

ratosthenes rolled up a book and placed it inside its cylinder tube. He set it on a table and rolled up another book. This one was also placed in a tube. When he was finished, Eratosthenes gathered the books in his arms and walked to the shelves to return them to their proper slots. As head of the library at Alexandria, in Ptolemy-controlled Egypt, this was a daily task. Eratosthenes was scholar — one of the greatest that Greek civilization had produced — and yet he enjoyed the daily tasks of keeping the library organized. It kept his mind free to wonder. He stepped up on a stool to slide a book onto a high shelf, took a deep breath of his surroundings, and smiled. As much work as it was to keep a library of this size in shape, he never tired of his job.

There was so much to learn. In his 70 plus years of living, Eratosthenes had questioned everything. How many stars are in the sky? How far away are the sun and the moon? How big around is the earth? For every question that had satisfactorily been answered, four more popped into his head. Spending his days surrounded by more than 500,000 books helped keep the questions at bay, for there was always another book to be read. Many of the volumes, Eratosthenes had written himself. Some were about mathematics, some were about geography, and some were even about poetry. He stepped down from his stool and glanced at the next book in his arms. From behind him he heard someone clear his throat.

"Good day Eratosthenes. I wonder if you would be so kind as to help me?" Eratosthenes turned around and looked down his nose at the middle aged man wearing a himation, a thin, long cloak that was loosely wrapped around his body. He sighed and said, "I suppose I could spare a few moments. What do you need Aristophanes of Byzantium?"

"I would like to work more with Aristotle's 'Nature of Animals.' I'm abridging it you know."

"Yes, I know. And?" questioned Eratosthenes.

"Oh, and…well you see. . ." Aristophanes cleared his throat again. "The truth is…"

"Please Aristophanes, get on with it. I am a busy man. I have my own research to conduct."

"Yes, yes of course you do. The truth is, I can't find it," Aristophanes finished in one breath.

"What?" snapped Eratosthenes, "What do you mean you can't find it? Have you looked on the shelf? Did you ask one of the other librarians for help?"

"Yes, yes of course I did. It was there yesterday, but

today it can't be found."

"Come with me," huffed Eratosthenes.

Eratosthenes led Aristophanes to the other side of the library where Aristotle's works were kept. Along the way he gave the books he was holding to another librarian with a terse, "Re-shelve these properly." At the correct shelf, Eratosthenes quickly looked through the books by Aristotle. Sure enough 'Nature of Animals" was missing. "Where were you using this book yesterday?" he asked.

Aristophanes pointed to a nearby table and the two men walked to it. "Let's sit down and retrace yesterday's steps," said Eratosthenes.

Aristophanes became thoughtful and then began to speak. "Hmmm, well, I remember I was also reading works from Homer, but I looked and I didn't mistakenly put 'Nature of Animals' away with those books."

"Can you remember anything else?" questioned Eratosthenes. "Who else have you been researching lately?"

"No one. I don't like to have too many projects going at a time. Except, perhaps, yes! I was reading Plato's dialogues this week. I have been thinking of splitting them into a trilogy."

"Then let us look under Plato's works and see what we can find."

The two men walked to Plato's section of the library and found the missing book. "Oh Eratosthenes, I am deeply embarrassed. I humbly beg your forgiveness for my thoughtlessness. To think I might have lost such a valuable book! I am sick thinking about it." Aristophanes looked up into Eratosthenes' stern face and was surprised to see the hint of a grin on his lips.

"Come Aristophanes, I think we will go for a walk." Eratosthenes put the wayward book back in its proper slot, then led the way out of the library and into a courtyard. They walked through magnificent columns and past a tranquil garden. As they passed through the Museum, the famous school of which the library was a part, Aristophanes wondered at his fate. On they walked until they came to a tower. The silent climb up the tower stairs had Aristophanes sweating from more than just exercise. They emerged at the top of the stairs at the astronomical observatory. The golden sun was high in the sky and the observatory was empty.

Eratosthenes gazed up into the heavens and then down at the city of Alexandria. He seemed to be lost in thought. Aristophanes grew more uncomfortable as the silence continued. "Do you remember the first time you saw the city?" Eratosthenes quietly asked.

Startled at the unexpected question, Aristophanes paused before answering. "Yes. Seeing the Pharos for the first time positively took my breath away. I couldn't wait for night to see the lighthouse in all its splendor. It was a magnificent sight."

"Many people come to Alexandria just to see the lighthouse. It is indeed amazing. When I first saw it, I marveled at its height, truly the tallest structure I have ever seen that was built by man. Gazing upon it made me love mathematics more than ever. I was thrilled to be in Alexandria, to start studying at the Museum and to start teaching. Ahh, the museum! — with its library, classrooms, lecture halls, parks, and zoo! That was so many years ago. Soon after my arrival, I was studying in the library. I was caught up in my research, and when I put my books away, I put them away improperly. When Zenodotus, the head librarian at the time, found out, I thought he was going to flay me alive." Eratosthenes paused to chuckle. "His system of arranging the books alphabetically had not been in place long. He did not appreciate a young upstart spoiling his new filing system." Eratosthenes really laughed now.

Aristophanes said, "I can imagine the look on his face."

Eratosthenes clapped a hand on Aristophanes' shoulder and said, "Do not trouble yourself over your mistake Aristophanes. I know what it is like to get lost in your scholarship and forget the time, the day and even where you are. You remembered in good time where the book was. There was no damage done."

"Thank you Eratosthenes, you are very kind. I had always understood your character to be haughty."

"To be sure, I am. Don't you allow anyone to think differently." Eratosthenes winked as he said this.

Aristophanes smiled and replied, "Your secret is safe with me, but truly, you could have told me this in the library. Why did you bring me up here?"

"I am an old man now. Someday a new librarian will be needed and I am inclined to submit your name for consideration. You showed great integrity today by admitting your mistake. A lesser man would have just left the library and allowed someone else to discover the error.

Aristophanes shook his head. "No. Never that. I could not live with myself if a book went missing indefinitely because of something I did. Especially a book I needed to finish my work." This time both men laughed.

"I have not been up on this tower in a long time," said Eratosthenes. "I thought it would be a good place for a private talk. Many years ago, when my knees were much more spry, Archimedes and I would frequently come here at night and study the stars. He was a great man, an Alpha."

"Clearly, Archimedes was number one in his field. You are as well; you must have also been known as Alpha."

Now it was Eratosthenes' turn to shake his head, "No, my friend. There you are wrong. I was a Beta."

"You? Second class? I can't accept that," said Aristophanes.

"No, not second class, just second in many fields. Unlike others, I could not settle into one discipline. I loved mathematics, astronomy, poetry, maps, the world, science. It is difficult to be first when one's interests lie in so many places. I was also called 'Pentathlos'."

"An athlete that competes in five different events?" asked Aristophanes.

"More like someone who is good at so many things."

"I see. So others call you Beta or Pentathlos. What do you call yourself?"

"I call myself Philologos, a friend of learning."

The two spent a few more minutes talking and then headed for the stairs again. On their way down Eratosthenes said, "I am enjoying our discussion, but I must continue my day. Will you join me in the baths?"

"I, too, am enjoying our discussion and I will gladly join you at the baths," replied Aristophanes.

The pair wandered to the gymnasium, not for exercise this time, but to enjoy the heated baths. After being stripped down and rubbed with oil, they climbed into sunken tubs filled with warm water. They relaxed and continued their conversation.

"You were born in Cyrene, like my teacher Callimachus, were you not?" asked Aristophanes.

"Yes I was. Callimachus was my grammar teacher here in Alexandria. He was a good poet and scholar. When I was a young boy, Lysanias of Cyrene was my teacher. When I grew of age, I went to Athens and studied under Ariston of Chios. He was a philosopher."

"And what brought you to Alexandria? To study?"

"The opportunity to study here was phenomenal, but as I mentioned before, I came to teach. I came at the request of Euergetes to be his son Philopator's tutor."

"Ptolemy III asked you here personally to teach his son? You tutored our current king, Ptolemy IV?" Aristophanes exclaimed.

Eratosthenes grinned. "Yes I did. It was a great honor. Especially since Euergetes later made me the head of the library. I am very grateful to the Ptolemies for establishing the library and museum here in Alexandria. It has been a great boon to scholars."

"Yes it has," Aristophanes agreed.

They settled back in their tubs and enjoyed a friendly conversation. Aristophanes delightedly told of his work with adding accent marks into the Greek language to help denote pronunciation. He also happily enjoyed editing classical

199

authors. Eratosthenes spoke of his passion for chronological lists. He had created a calendar with leap years and had made a history of the world back to the time of Troy. He also loved maps; maps of the earth and maps of the heavens. He told Aristophanes in great detail of the map he had made of the Nile River all the way to Khartoum. He was even more excited as he described the map he had made of the known world.

This led him to describe the system he had devised for longitude and latitude lines. He was so enthusiastic about his subject and a willing set of listening ears, that he launched into his creation of the armillary, or celestial sphere—a ball representing the earth with a skeleton of graduated metal circles around it which was used to demonstrate the motion of the stars around the earth. From there he jumped straight into his star catalogue.

Armillary   Sphere

"It has 675 stars. Imagine! There are 675 stars in the sky that have been properly catalogued. In my poem 'Hermes'…"

"Enough Eratosthenes!" laughed Aristophanes. "I have read your astronomical poem. It is amazing. Haughty indeed. They should tell of how loquacious you are. You truly are a friend of learning. Now, I am wrinkled beyond recognition and my stomach tells me it is past the dinner hour."

"A fine idea, a fine idea. Let us go to the agora for dinner." Aristophanes agreed. They dressed and left the gymnasium.

The agora, or marketplace, was still very busy in the late afternoon. Different groups had gathered to hear speakers, and as far as the eye could see, merchants were selling their wares. Anything could be purchased in the agora. There were linens and papyrus from Egypt, spices from Syria, ivory from Africa, dates and wheat from Phoenicia, rugs from Persia, different cheeses from Gaul and Syracuse, iron ore from Elba, local fruits and vegetables, vases, armor, pottery, honey, olive oil and so much more. The agora was a feast for the eyes. The food tantalized the nose. In one corner there was a slave auction taking place. Everywhere there were men shopping, talking, listening and debating.

Eratosthenes and Aristophanes stopped at different stalls to purchase bread and fruit. Then they found a low wall next to a tree to sit on and eat their meal. The shade from the tree kept them cool as they ate. Between bites, the men continued their discourse. "I would like to know more about your sieve," Aristophanes said.

"My sieve is most wonderful. I invented an algorithm, a procedure for accomplishing some task, to find prime numbers. A prime number as you know is a number that cannot be evenly divided except by itself and the number one. For example, the number ten cannot be a prime number because it can evenly be divided by five or two as well as by ten and one. However, the number thirteen is a prime number because…it really is quite simple, let me show you."

"I don't know if anything is ever 'quite simple' with you, but please, do show me," said Aristophanes.

Eratosthenes turned behind him and broke off a small tree branch. He then used the branch to quickly draw numbers in the sandy dirt at his feet. He circled the number two and said, "Two is a prime number, which is why I circled it, and it is our starting point. Next we want to cross out all multiples of two." Eratosthenes deftly crossed out the numbers 4, 6, 8, and 10. "Basically all the even numbers are no longer counted. Two is the only even prime number. Do you understand?"

"Yes, I am with you so far," replied Aristophanes.

"Good. Next we find the next non-crossed out number, in this case it is three. Three is a prime number. We circle it. Now we need to cross out all the multiples of three. That would be six, which is already crossed out, nine, twelve, also crossed out, then fifteen and so on."

"Oh, I see, let me try the next set," begged Aristophanes.

"By all means." Eratosthenes gave his stick to Aristophanes.

"Alright, two and three are primes, four is crossed out, the next number is five," Aristophanes said. "I'm going to circle five then cross out the multiples of five. Let me think, hmmm, ten and fifteen and twenty are already crossed off. I need to mark out twenty-five, thirty is already taken care of, and thirty-five. Oh wow, this is fun! Now to start at the beginning, six is our next number, but already crossed out, so our next number is seven."

Aristophanes circled seven and then crossed out multiples of seven. He worked quietly for a few minutes and

then stopped. "So, the first ten prime numbers are: 2, 3, 5, 7, 11, 13, 17, 19, 23 and 29."

"Excellent work! Not only are you a scholar, but a budding mathematician, Eratosthenes said.

"I never knew I had such mathematical abilities in me. Very clever. What a wonderful thing you have created. I will show my colleagues tomorrow."

"Careful, Aristophanes, or more than just Homer will call to you in the library. You may find yourself in Euclid's section," chuckled Eratosthenes.

Aristophanes laughed with him. "I can see why being a Beta would be an honor and not an insult. There is so much to learn and discover, even without Homer." Aristophanes used the stick to wipe out the math lesson, then tossed the stick over his shoulder. He stood up, stretched and yawned. Eratosthenes copied him. They began to walk, enjoying the sights and sounds of the agora. Merchants were beginning to pack their wares for the evening. A cool breeze from the Mediterranean Sea blew through the stalls and rustled their clothing.

"This has been such an excellent afternoon, I hate for it to end," Aristophanes said.

"Then accompany me home and we can share some wine this evening," Eratosthenes offered.

Aristophanes readily agreed, and the short walk to Eratosthenes' home was spent in companionable musings. They entered Eratosthenes' home directly into the andron, the entertaining area. They sat on cushions around a low table. Calling for a house slave, Eratosthenes ordered wine for himself and his guest. The slave observed this would be a night for scholarly pursuits; so he liberally watered the wine before returning to his master. It would never do to become intoxicated when in deep discussion. The slave left the flagon of wine and two cups on the table. Outside the sun had set and the moon was rising. Another slave brought a lighted olive oil lamp to the table to dispel the darkness. They relaxed with their wine and slowly resumed talking.

"Eratosthenes, you have done and seen much. Your remarkable brain has thought more than probably ten ordinary men. What do you consider to be your best work, your most important accomplishment?"

"I measured the earth."

"Indeed? Tell me about it," said Aristophanes.

"We know that the earth is round," explained Eratosthenes. "It is not flat, nor does it rest on the back of a turtle. It is a sphere."

"Agreed."

"And since it is a sphere, it must have a beginning and an ending, but how large does that make it? I had to know. Many have guessed. Many have deduced, but I truly measured the earth."

"That is quite a claim. How did you go about it?" asked Aristophanes.

"It all comes down to simple geometry," replied Eratosthenes. "Many years ago, I heard of a well in Syene, which is south of here on the Nile River. Every year at noon on the summer solstice, the sun shines all the way down to the bottom of this well. Imagine being able to see all the way to the bottom of a deep well. It made me think — and I had to know — what about the wells in Alexandria? Would I be able to see all the way to the bottom? Waiting for the summer solstice that year was very difficult. Right before noon, I was ready and waiting over the top of a well. And what do you think happened? I could not see all the way to the bottom of my well; there was a shadow cast by the sun's rays. Naturally, I asked why? Why does my well have a shadow and not the well in Syene? It occurred to me that the sun was directly over the well in Syene at noon, but not directly over my well in Alexandria at the exact same time. How could this be? It goes back to the earth being a sphere. When we look around, the ground seems flat, but really, all of the earth is curved. It was because of this curve that my well was shadowed and Syene's was not."

"That's all very well and good, but what does it mean?" asked Aristophanes.

"Patience, Aristophanes. After all, I had to wait much, much longer for all of my measurements. I knew I needed to measure the angle of my shadow here in Alexandria. I did this by tapping a straight stick into the ground. With simple geometry, I measured the angle of the shadow at just over seven degrees. Seven degrees is 1/50 of a circle. All I needed to know now was how much distance there was between Alexandria and Syene and multiply that measurement by 50 to give me the full distance around the earth."

"Ingenious!" exclaimed Aristophanes, "How did you measure the distance between the two cities? Did you use camels?"

"I would have liked to use camels, but they do not take even steps. Plus they stop and start without any consideration to mathematical figures. No, I needed a much more accurate figure. I hired a walker to do it for me."

"Did you use the king's bematists?" asked Aristophanes.

"Precisely. I was able to use a few of the king's official road surveyors. They were very good at their job. With their information, the calculation of the earth's circumference became perfectly easy. The only thing that puzzles me now is what the rest of the earth looks like. We have mapped the land, but there is still a lot of earth left over. I believe the rest of the earth must be filled with an interconnected ocean."

"That seems logical enough to me," Aristophanes said. "So just how big is the earth?"

"It is 252,000 stadia. The distance between Alexandria and Syene is 5,000 stadia. My shadow was about 7 degrees, which is 1/50 of the circle. By multiplying 5,000 by 50 we have the number 250,000. I feel I must admit that I did add an extra 2,000 to this number to come up with 252,000 stadia. This number was much easier to work with. A circle has 360 degrees. 252,000 is easily divisible by 360 and 60. And there you have it, the circumference of the earth," said Eratosthenes.

"Perfectly simple," agreed Aristophanes. "I wish I had thought of it myself. I never realized numbers could be so simple. Plato's saying is correct, 'Let no man destitute of geometry enter my doors.'"

"Yes, we would be nowhere without our geometry. It has kept me busy these many years."

Aristophanes raised his cup to Eratosthenes. "Here's to letting it keep you busy for many years to come."

"Thank you Aristophanes, I will drink to that."

They drank their wine and talked for a few more hours. When Aristophanes returned to his own home, the moon was very high in the sky. He gazed at the moon and smiled. *"I bet Eratosthenes even knows how far away the moon is,"* he thought. He walked home through the cool night air and reflected on his day. His day had begun with a mistake and had ended in rapture. Aristophanes felt changed, as if he were better somehow. He knew that he had dined with greatness today and hoped to ever remember that feeling. He walked a little taller and smiled a little broader as he continued on his way home.

Excerpt of a letter from Aristophanes of Byzantium to his student Aristarchos of Samothrace dated 195 B.C.

...Eratosthenes died this last week. He was in his 80th year. Although I spent but one afternoon with him long ago, his influence still rests upon me. He called himself Philologos, a friend of learning. I must agree, for he was well versed in astronomy, mathematics, geography (a term he himself coined), science, writing, poetry, and the list continues. Lovingly referred to as Beta, the great Archimedes dismissed this attitude and proclaimed his friend an Alpha, or number one in his own right. After my extraordinary afternoon in Eratosthenes' presence, I agree with Archimedes' assessment. Eratosthenes was born asking questions and spent his whole life trying to answer them. He left the world a better, more intelligent place than when he came into it.

I am to be appointed librarian in his stead. If he ever submitted my name for consideration, I may never know. I do know that I am grateful for the opportunity. May I continue in his footsteps and keep the library and his writings safe for all to learn from. I will ever remember my day with him. May his learning and knowledge go forth and nourish the earth. Let the world know of his remarkable accomplishments and may they never forget...

Epilogue

Sadly, most of the work of Eratosthenes (275-195 B.C.) is lost today. We mainly know of his accomplishments through the works of other authors whose books have survived. With today's technology we have been able to more accurately measure the circumference of the earth, but Eratosthenes was very close to the actual figure. He said the earth was 252,000 stadia. There is much debate today over how long a stadium (singular for stadia) was. The best guesses put the 252,000 stadia equal to either 24,390 miles or to 24,662 miles. With either figure, Eratosthenes was only off by 200-400 miles! Quite an accomplishment for two thousand years ago.

Although the afternoon that Eratosthenes and Aristophanes spent together is fiction, Aristophanes of Byzantium (not to be confused with the playwright Aristophanes) was a real person and did in fact become the next librarian after Eratosthenes. What the story tells of Aristophanes' life is also true. Eratosthenes and Aristophanes did know each other and could have spent an afternoon together talking about their lives. They lived in Hellenistic Greece and what they did and where they went were things people really did in those days. In his letter, Aristophanes writes to Aristarchos of Samothrace who truly was his student, who would in turn become head librarian after Aristophanes died.

About the Author

Susannah Rice currently lives in
the state of Virginia but has lived
in many locations across the United
States. She and her five children
have enjoyed exploring the beauty of
America and learning about her rich
history as they homeschool together.
Susannah enjoys hiking with her
family as well as directing and acting

in plays. However, her main passion is books. Whether it is
reading to herself or to her children, or writing her own stories,
you can often find Susannah somewhere within the pages of a
book.

To my dear family, Barb, Susan and the HiC Ladies.
I thank God for your encouragement and support.

Constantine
By This Sign, You Shall Conquer

by Jocelyn James

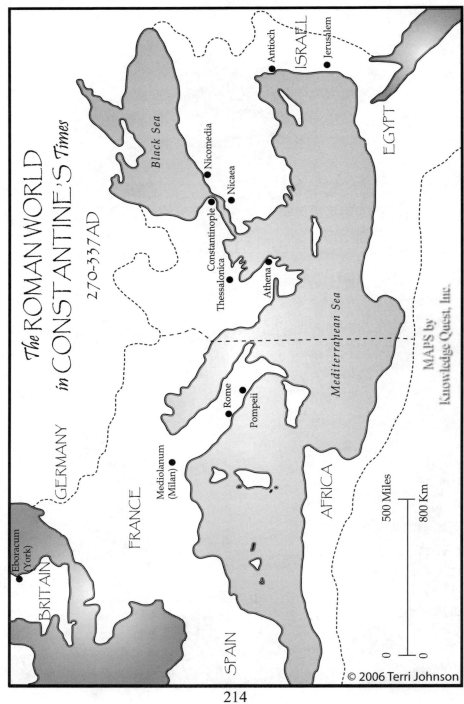

The ROMAN WORLD in CONSTANTINE'S *Times*
270-337AD

Black Sea

ISRAEL

Antioch

Jerusalem

EGYPT

Nicomedia

Nicaea

Constantinople

Thessalonica

Athena

Mediterranean Sea

Rome

Pompeii

Mediolanum
(Milan)

GERMANY

FRANCE

BRITAIN

Eboracum
(York)

SPAIN

AFRICA

500 Miles

800 Km

0

0

MAPS by
Knowledge Quest, Inc.

© 2006 Terri Johnson

8
Constantine
By this Sign, You shall Conquer

by Jocelyn James

 He awoke suddenly with the vision still vivid in his mind. He looked around his tent and saw that the light was starting to seep between the cracks in the skins and the wall hangings. He knew the sentry by his door would not disturb him for a while. In the half-light, he lay back pondering the scene yet again. The apostle Paul had an encounter with Christ on the road to Damascus. Could he be so blessed? The vision of the cross was before him and the words upon it, which had pierced his soul: *In Hoc Signo Vinces* — "By this sign, you shall conquer."

This was the confirmation he needed to affirm his course. He believed he had the sanction of the Christian God, and would fight in His name.

~~~~~

It was 28 October 312 AD. Here at Saxa Ruba, a little north of Rome, would be the ultimate fight to see who would become the Emperor of the western world. Until that day, Constantine had been confident in his abilities and had the unswerving support of his men. Leaving his tent, Constantine went to survey the field before the coming battle. He saw a formidable force assembled. There was an army three times the size of his own, comprised of the whole Praetorian Guard. How could he be victorious against such overwhelming odds, against the best soldiers of Rome?

He saw the cross again in his mind, blazing in the light, reminding him of his certain victory. Constantine hurriedly gave instructions for Christian symbols to be painted on as many helmets and shields as was possible. A tall P and small x were painted on a cross and this emblem became the new banner under which they would fight.

The battle itself was furious. The Praetorian Guard, the peak body of Rome's fighting men, did not give way, but their ranks were cut down where they stood. Maxentius, who had dared to challenge Constantine, tried to escape by crossing the Milvian Bridge over the Tiber River and drowned. It was a momentous victory for Constantine. Now as master of the western world, Constantine gave thanks to the true light that had helped him.

~~~~~

Perhaps when his father was promoted from prefect of Gaul to Caesar of the western realm, it appeared that

216

Constantine himself was destined for greatness. That time, however, had brought about one of the saddest periods of his life. He remembered his mother's sorrow:

"Mother, why are you upset?" he asked.

"Flavius Valerius Constantinus – are you spying on me?" Helena chastened. Constantine had entered the garden normally reserved for his mother in their palatial prefect's residence.

"Mother, do you have to call me by my full name? Have I done something wrong?" Constantine looked at her, somewhat anxiously.

"No, my son. Come here and sit by me. You must hear this soon anyway." Constantine sat on the stone bench near his mother. "Your father has been promoted – he is to be Caesar of the western realm."

"That's good, isn't it?" Constantine ventured.

"Well, yes, it is very good for his career. He is still under Diocletian though – you understand that?" she asked.

"Yes. I know that Empire is ruled by four men. The two Augusti emperors are higher than the Caesars; but Diocletian, Augustus of the East, is really the one who is head over all," Constantine replied.

"Then you will know that whatever Diocletian commands, must be obeyed," Helena said, simply.

"Yes..." he responded tentatively.

"Diocletian has ordered that your father is to marry Theodora, stepdaughter of Maximian."

"How can he do that – he's married to you!"

"We are to be divorced, my son," she quavered momentarily, and then regained the composure in her voice.

"You see why this must be so? Maximian is Augustus of the West and this binds your father to him and Diocletian. It will ensure his loyalty and peace for the Empire."

Constantine coiled back in shock. He could not think of the good of the Empire right now. His mind and his heart rebelled.

"Flavius, you are only 12. One day you will see that this is a sacrifice that is worth making."

He was not really listening to her; his mind was still churning it over.

"What is going to happen to us, mother?" he asked with uncertainty.

"You will be going to join Diocletian's forces, where you will no doubt become a fine soldier," she replied. "I am going away into the country, but will not be far from you."

"So I am to insure father's loyalty, too, by being a hostage of Diocletian?" Constantine retorted angrily. He looked across at his mother's serene face and his anger subsided. "Mother, how can you sit there so calmly, telling me all of this?"

Helena sighed. "I have found it hard. You saw I was upset when you came into the garden but I am learning to accept it. I love you and your father and now this is what is best for you." She reached over and held his hand. "I think it is also because of the Christians I see. They always seem so calm even though they suffer greatly at times. What is my pain in comparison?"

"You have not become a Christian, have you, mother?" Constantine enquired accusingly.

"Would it be so terrible if I have?" she asked. " No, son.

218

I am drawn to their teachings and their lives, but I am not a Christian."

"I am glad, mother. You know they do strange things."

"If you came to one of their services with me, you might think differently. There is no time for that now. You are to be escorted to Diocletian tomorrow."

~~~~~

Constantine spent the next ten years in the service of Diocletian. He learned how to fight both on the battlefield and also in the realm of politics. He learned to survive in a world of power-hungry men all vying to be the next Caesar or the next Augustus. Constantine became a good bodyguard for Diocletian, and in turn, he, too, was protected. Galerius, the ambitious Caesar of the East, was his main rival. Galerius wanted more than the title of Augustus. He desired to become the sole ruler of the whole Empire.

Galerius was in charge of the campaign to put down the rebellious Persians in the East. At first, the campaign had been a failure. Galerius had made the age-old mistake of thrusting straight through to the heart of the Persian camp instead of coming at them through Armenia. Constantine and his reinforcements had arrived too late to help gain the victory, but had cleaned up the Persians from behind as they tried to pursue Galerius' retreating forces. It had been a humiliation for Galerius and was seen as a victory for the young and able Constantine.

By this time, Constantine had become an imposing figure. His father had been nicknamed "Chlorus", meaning pale, and although Constantine bore great resemblance to his father, he was not quite as fair in complexion. His mother was Greek and some of her coloring had found its way to him. He had become broad and solid in his years of military training, and he was very tall. He now entered Diocletian's court with a confident manner and presence. Diocletian liked this young man, with his incisive mind and feel for battle. He had summoned Constantine to talk with him about Galerius.

"Dominus, you sent for me?" Constantine said. He always addressed Diocletian by that old and revered title.

"I wanted to tell you that Galerius has been sent out again on another campaign against the Persians."

"What is my assignment, my lord?" Constantine asked.

"You are to stay here in Antioch and guard my wife and my daughter," Diocletian commanded.

"Dominus, I thought…"

"No, Constantine. You distinguished yourself, perhaps a little too much, in the last battle. Galerius must not be given any excuses to sideline you. Besides, yours is an important mission. My wife and daughter have Christian sympathies, as you know. I need them to be guarded carefully in this turbulent time."

"Am I to prohibit them from meeting with other Christians?" Constantine enquired.

"No, I don't think even I could stop them from doing that! I know you would prefer to be in battle, but this is more important. Galerius will be victorious this time and will try to gain power for himself. I need my best people to be close to me and close to my family."

"Yes, Dominus." Constantine saluted and then left him.

Diocletian had been right when he said the task would not be easy. The women were in Christian company for a good part of each day. Constantine would have to be with them all the time, in all the meetings; they were not to leave his sight.

"I think you are becoming attracted to the Christian teachings as well, Constantinus," Diocletian's wife said to him one day.

"Augusta, this God does seem to be powerful, and my mother has always been drawn to Christian people. But I will not become a Christian. I think you know why," he replied. "I am surprised at both you and your daughter. You know that Caesar Galerius would like nothing better than to crush the Christians. He sees them as a menace in the Empire. Your daughter is his wife, and she is so overt in her Christian beliefs! Gaius has almost convinced my lord to punish them."

"We are not afraid if persecution should come," she replied with a sense of resolve in her voice.

~~~~~

The persecution did come, though it did not touch Diocletian's family. In 303, Diocletian signed an order for the persecution of Christians. There was a reign of terror in which countless Christian churches, buildings, and homes were destroyed. Many Christians were sent to the arena to die, and the sight of it all sickened Constantine. The one heartening thing for Constantine was hearing that his father had not fully enforced the decree in Gaul. He had inflicted only minimal damage upon Christians.

The turmoil had only just begun when, in 305, Diocletian abdicated from his 20-year rule as Augustus. He made sure that Maximian in the West did so as well. Constantine's father was promoted to the position of Augustus, as was Galerius. Speculation became rife as to who would get the junior positions of Caesar under them. Perhaps many felt that Constantine should rule under his father, but Diocletian was not in favour of family dynasties. Constantine and one other, Maxentius, the son of Maximian, were left out in the cold.

That did not trouble Constantine much, as he had other concerns. Galerius had always felt threatened by the young man and now Diocletian was not there to protect Constantine. Constantine knew he had to get away. Constantius Chlorus had asked for his son to join him some months after the coronation. He was failing in health and wanted to see Constantine again before he died. It was the last thing that Galerius wanted – what would happen if Chlorus died and Constantine was there by his side?

Eventually, after some delays, Constantine was allowed to go. He had hard months of travel ahead of him to reach his father. Constantius Chlorus had been fighting in Britannia against the Picts, and it was in Eboracum (York) that Constantine finally met up with him.

After a short period of time fighting alongside his son, Constantius Chlorus finally became too weak to keep going. When he died in 306, all the men proclaimed Constantine as their new Augustus. Constantine readily accepted this elevation and the news sent shockwaves through the Empire.

One man saw the time was ripe for an alliance with

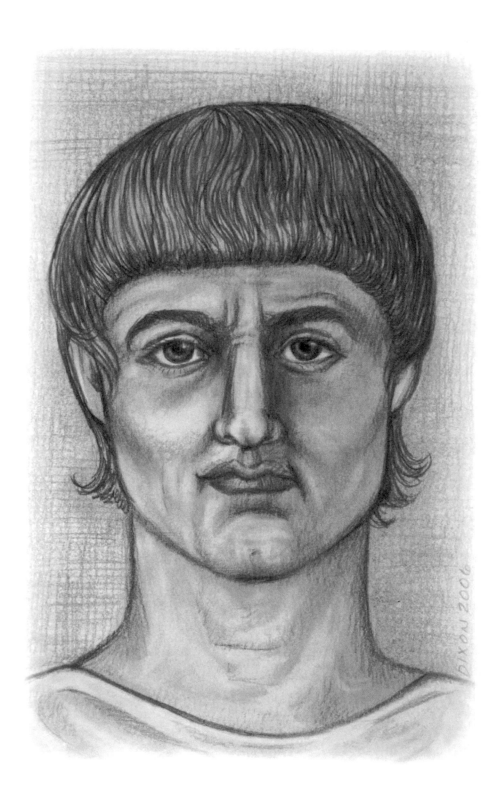

Constantine – Maximian. He had arranged for his daughter, Fausta, to be Constantine's wife many years before. Now was the time to forge the alliance so Constantine and Fausta wed in Gaul soon after his promotion.

There was not much time to enjoy married life as Constantine then spent the next 5 years constantly on the move with his army. His rivals may have changed around him, but the power struggle remained. When Constantine was finally on his approach to Rome to fight against his brother-in-law, Maxentius, he knew that this momentous battle could have only one victor. He had been surprised when his scouts informed him that Maxentius had left the safe walls of Rome to meet him in battle and had boats crossing the width of the Tiber near the Milvian Bridge. Perhaps that was the first encouraging sign of divine favour. When he had the vision of the cross, he was sure the Christian God had blessed him in the battle.

~~~~~

Months had passed since that day when Constantine had rode into Rome victorious. As life descended from the dizzying heights of triumph, Constantine became restless again. Perhaps in the days of Caesar Augustus, when Rome was at its pinnacle, it would have been a sight to behold. Now, the buildings and monuments, once its glory, seemed hollow and shabby. The Senate had bestowed honours upon him and even agreed to erect a triumphal arch, but the Senators were too fixed in their ideas and the city was suffocating in its paganism. He knew he had to leave.

Licinius, who had become the sole ruler of the East, had

agreed to come to Mediolanum (Milan) for a peace treaty with Constantine. In return for Constantine's protection, Licinius agreed to a joint declaration, which came to be known as the Edict of Milan. It proclaimed that the persecution of Christians and Christianity would be halted throughout all of the Empire. Now they could worship God freely, without fear and with the protection and blessing of the Emperors. It was a monumental change and led the whole Empire into a pro-Christian stance.

This agreement was sealed with the marriage of Constantine's half sister, Constantia to Licinius. Apart from Constantine's court, his family also joined him for this event. It had been sometime since he had last seen Crispus, his son, but he was startled to see the changes in him.

Crispus was becoming a fine young man with a very fair appearance. In many ways he was reminiscent of his grandfather, Constantius Chlorus. He had started his military training and now stood in his dress attire. He was laughing and talking with Fausta at the outdoor reception. Constantine was happy that his young wife had made Crispus feel welcome, even though he was not her own son. The two of them were actually quite close in age as Fausta was only 19.

Constantine made his way over to Crispus and Fausta.

"Crispus, you have grown again while I have been away," Constantine remarked encouragingly before Crispus could speak.

"Thank you, father," he replied. "I have heard of your great victories and cannot wait until I can join you in battle. Do you think that there will be some left by the time I can fight?" he said, eagerly.

His father laughed. "I believe there will always be battles to be had and I am sure you will get your opportunity in time." He was bemused as he thought of how he, too, longed for battle at the same age. "For now, I want your training to include other things. I have hired a Christian tutor to instruct you in the faith I have now taken."

"As you wish, father," he replied. Fausta had been listening while this conversation took place. She was small next to these men, but showed a dignity befitting the purple Augusta robe she wore. She was less adorned than Constantine, who liked to wear jewels and be prominent at public occasions.

He turned and looked at Fausta. "I wish my entire household to have instruction in the Christian faith – you and our children when they are able."

"Of course, my lord," Fausta replied. She did not really mind which god she was to serve, as long as he fit into her plans. She wanted nothing less than power for herself and her own children.

Constantine felt satisfied. He knew that he would need more instruction himself, as he knew little about Christian beliefs. He had faced stiff opposition from the Senators in Rome and needed orators around him. Already, he was seeking learned Christian men join him.

Now that it was an honour to be a Christian in Constantine's court, many people, especially those wanting advancement, suddenly became Christians too. This didn't concern Constantine. He believed that this would aid and strengthen his ambitions for a new Christian Empire, and didn't worry too much about the sincerity of those who had had a change of heart.

~~~~~

The next 10 years were not as peaceful as many expected them to be. Licinius became threatened by the prominence of Christians in his part of the empire. Constantine seemed to know no borders and aided them no matter where they were. He built churches in Rome and the East, he sent aid and even claimed that he had a divine mission from God to help Christians everywhere.

The friction finally became too great as Constantine and Licinius now battled for rule of the whole realm. Constantine felt he was justified, as he needed to defend the faith no matter where it led him. He really wanted to extend and expand the Empire and make it a Christian one. It was the vision of the cross and the glory of Christ that led him on and all he did was justified by it – whether truly in God's name or not.

The final battle with Licinius saw Constantine chasing him back towards Byzantium. Crispus, now about 23, was in command of the naval forces and had his father's keen abilities for strategy and command. He had already won several battles both in Gaul and against the German barbarians. He was sure to distinguish himself in battle here, too.

Constantine and Crispus looked over the maps of the coming battle in Constantine's tent one evening.

"I want you to lead the attack on Licinius' fleet tomorrow." Constantine said resolutely.

"It seems a bold plan, father. Licinius has superior numbers. If he should turn and strike back at us, we might not recover from the blow," Crispus cautioned.

"I believe these plans are sound. It is precisely because Licinius does not expect it that I think we will be successful. While we have been waiting here, more of our ships have come in to reinforce your fleet. I can sense that he is anxious and on the run. He will throw himself behind those walls at Byzantium and then we will have him," Constantine said firmly.

"Alright, father. I, too, would have it no other way. We shall prepare for the attack, and with the helps of the gods, your path will be clear," Crispus replied.

"With the help of one God, Crispus. Have you been instructed for nothing?" Constantine sighed and placed his hand on his son's shoulder. "I would have no other person lead this sea engagement."

"Thank you, father," Crispus said with appreciation, and then walked out into the night.

~~~~~

Crispus devastated Licinius' fleet over the next days, leaving Licinius to find refuge within the walls of the Byzantium. Constantine was now able to provision his fleet from the Black Sea and starve his enemy within the city with a long siege.

It was during the Siege of Byzantium that Constantine began to see the advantages of this location. He marvelled that no other site was so well defended by nature. This Greek city had the benefit of being at the tip of Europe. It was surrounded on two sides by sea and was well fortified around its perimeter by thick walls. The city itself was built on hilly terrain, making any attack on land extremely difficult. Over hundreds of years many others had come to conquer this ancient city. The most famous of these was Philip of Macedon, Alexander's father. Their attempts had been to no avail – Byzantium had survived each onslaught.

It took all of Constantine's ingenuity to break into the city. He constructed mounds of earth equal in height to the ramparts of Byzantium. Lofty towers were then erected from which great stones and darts were hurled at the enemy. Battering rams shook the walls in many places, and finally Constantine broke through and was victorious. To make sure of his victory, Licinius, who had escaped during the siege, was pursued and stripped of the right to wear the purple robe of an Augustus. Unfortunately, this was not enough for Constantine and he had Licinius executed a year later on charges of treason.

After years of struggle, the whole Empire was united under one ruler, Constantine the First. He had vanquished his rivals. He had made his Empire prosperous and successful. It was while he slept within the walls of Byzantium that he had another dream: a vision to make this place his capital, Constantine's city, Constantinople.

~~~~~

Constantine looked around at the holes in the walls that would need repair. He was here with his architects and surveyors to look over the work to be done. Dressed in all his finery and with a lance in his hand, Constantine started to pace out the dimensions he wanted for his new city. His officials walked behind him, taking measurements and writing down notes of where the key buildings were to go. As Constantine kept walking, his officials began to get anxious.

"How much further, Dominus?" they enquired, trying to remain reverent.

"I shall advance until He, the invisible Guide who marches before me, sees fit for me to stop," Constantine replied.

He walked on until the city, which once only filled in the tip of the horn, now filled in a large triangle of land. Constantine was not content to have a city as good as Rome, it had to be larger and better. Architects, builders and craftsmen now poured in from all over the Empire to begin the work. The finest materials, jewels and resources were bought with the new coin that Constantine had made for the Empire – one of pure gold and each coin of equal weight and value. Eventually it would be known as the "Bezant" as it was from Byzantium.

Constantine had to leave this vision in the hands of his builders and keep on with the task of building his Empire. He ran his court from Nicomedia, as Diocletian had done so many years before. It was a mere 80 miles from Constantinople, enabling Constantine to keep an eye on the building progress.

Now that Constantine was the sole ruler of the Empire, he could bring in reforms for the benefit of the whole realm. Christians in the West had been given their own special day to worship their God. Constantine proclaimed that the pagan day of the Sun was also a Christian day and thus Sunday became the Lord's Day for all Christian people. He made laws based on Christian principles, even though some of the punishments were harsh. He also established Christian courts and tightly bound the governing of the church with his role as supreme ruler over all.

As head of the church, he called a Council in 325. Debate was raging through the church about the nature of Christ and threatening to tear it apart, when Constantine called all the learned bishops of the church to meet at Nicaea.

Constantine appeared before the assembly in his glittering tiara and long purple robes. Around 250 bishops, mainly from the East of the Empire, rose at his entrance. They were unaccustomed to such displays of wealth as so many lived in very basic surroundings.

"Please be seated," Constantine began. "Though I too am a bishop appointed by God, I have come to learn and to listen so that we may divine the will of God together on this matter."

After countless daily sittings and arguments about the finer points of God's nature, much of which Constantine did not understand, his patience wore thin.

"This is enough! There will be no more discussion on the matter. You will come to an agreement. I want to see a statement of belief that can be proclaimed throughout the Empire."

Athanasius rose to address him, "My lord, we are not unanimous in our position. I do not believe that Arius and his followers will agree to say that Christ is of the same being and substance as the Father."

Eusebius of Caesarea then came forward and said, "Dominus, I have a creed we use in my church which I believe most here would readily accept."

It was read and most gave verbal assent. The council discussed some changes. After looking through it himself, Constantine suggested a few additions as well. Eventually, the following creed was agreed upon by the majority of bishops:

We believe in one God, the Father Almighty, Maker of all things visible and invisible, and in one Lord Jesus Christ, the Son of God, begotten of the Father, only-begotten, that is, of the same essence as the Father, God of God, and Light of Light, very God of very God...; by whom all things were made, both in heaven and on earth. Who for us men and our salvation was made flesh and lived among men, and suffered, and rose again the third day and ascended to the Father, and will come again in glory to judge the living and the dead. And we believe also in one Holy Spirit.

"Yes," said Constantine resolutely. "This is the will of God."

Arius and some of his followers refused to sign the creed, despite urgings to do so. Constantine exiled Arius and the other dissenting bishops, and made sure all of Arius' writings were burned. Unity in the church had to be safe guarded above all else.

~~~~~

Almost a year had passed since Constantine left Nicaea, and now, what should have been one of the happiest days of his life, was scarred by memories of the recent past.

When Constantine went to Rome to celebrate his 20th anniversary as Emperor, the Roman people had greeted him enthusiastically. This man was a mystery to them, an oriental looking ruler who was visiting them with all the pomp befitting the occasion. The procession was to go along the Sacred Way, past Constantine's Triumphal Arch, through the Forum and then on to the Temple of Jupiter on the Capitoline Hill. There, Constantine was to offer the customary sacrifice to Jupiter.

It began as all ceremonies of state should - Constantine was flanked by his bodyguards and religious leaders and making his way through the streets. As he walked along, waving to the crowd, taking in their adulation, he became overcome with grief. Fausta was not there to share in this celebration and neither was Crispus. Thoughts of them filled his mind, overcame his being – he struggled to go on. Why had they betrayed him? Had Crispus really meant to bring him down or was it the work of Fausta, who had accused this beloved son of treachery?

He felt anger, grief and shame – he had ordered their deaths en route from Nicomedia. No matter what he felt now, their deaths could not be undone. Constantine stopped and wept. He could not go on with the ceremony and did not even try. When he regained some composure, he turned to his advisers and said, "We are leaving now."

It was the darkest chapter of his life, and one he refused to talk about from that day on. Constantine returned to Nicomedia, to the disappointment of the Romans, and never returned.

Crispus and Fausta were to be erased from public memory, too. Once Constantine was back at court, he ordered all statues of Crispus to have his name chiselled off, and for all public records containing their names to be destroyed. Constantine could not bear to have any reminder of this episode in his life.

Constantine's mother, Helena, was also overcome with grief. She had come to live with his family again after he took up residence in Nicomedia. She had become a devout Christian and was worried about Constantine's conduct. Had he done something that would put his soul in jeopardy? She went to see Constantine soon after he returned from Rome.

"Constantine, I must speak with you," she said firmly.

"Yes, mother, please come in," Constantine replied.

"You know how upset I have been about Crispus and..." she began.

"I told you I don't want to discuss that," Constantine broke in, abruptly. His anger seemed to rise to the surface very quickly these days.

"I know, dear. I want to go to Jerusalem. I want to make a pilgrimage to the Holy City and see the sacred sites and find true spiritual rest for my soul." Helena knew she wanted this peace as much for Constantine as for herself.

Constantine sighed. "Of course, you may. Perhaps you can pray for me while you are there too. I almost wish I could go with you."

"I certainly will pray for you, my son," she added as she bade him farewell.

Constantine not only let Helena go on her pilgrimage, he gave her vast sums of money to ensure that Christian shrines and sacred sites were being cared for. Churches were built on some of these sites and Helena sent back relics to be displayed in the Constantine's court.

~~~~~

One final goal was before Constantine – to create his new city, the epitome of his Christian Empire. The work had been progressing well and was nearing completion. Like Rome, it was a city built on seven hills. The forums, the baths, palaces, columns and churches were to be more numerous and luxurious than the old city. The Circus Maximus in Rome was a large venue for chariot races and entertainments. Constantine's Hippodrome was to be at least twice the size and more regal and prestigious. It was lined with famous ancient monuments that had been taken from all over the Empire.

He had built St Peter's Cathedral for the church in Rome but he had plans for an even bigger church, St Sophia, in the heart of his New Rome. It would be elevated and dominate the skyline. The wealth of his Empire would adorn it and no one could doubt that God would make his dwelling there.

The marble, gold, and precious stones made the city dazzle in the sun. This city spoke of wealth, power and success. Finally, in 330, it was officially opened and dedicated. Constantine had a huge statue of himself, fashioned from one of Apollo, put into the forum. There was no doubting that the building of this city was his work, and he was claiming divine inspiration for it. For Constantine, this marked a new beginning and a rededication to the Christian God. He strived to make this city the greatest in the world.

~~~~~

"Dominus, I thank you for your hospitality," remarked a Roman Senator one evening. He had been dining at Constantine's palace at Constantinople and had been treated like royalty himself.

"I trust you will find yourself at home while you are in our immortal city. I am sure you will see my way of things and join us here." Constantine replied.

"My lord, I will give you my answer soon. Once I have seen my family again, I will give you my undertaking," he replied.

Constantine had a twinkle in his eye, "I will be hearing from you shortly, then," he mused.

The baffled Senator left the residence knowing it would be several months before he could settle his affairs in Rome and then even think about moving his family. His escort came to take him back to his lodgings in Constantinople. As the sedan chair wound through the streets, it seemed to take a lot longer to reach its destination.

"We are here, my lord," called out the slave.

He drew aside the curtains and stepped from the chair into a dream – here was a villa that was just like his own in Rome. The gardens were manicured in exactly the same fashion. Suddenly, from the top of the steps, he saw his wife and children. Wasn't he in Constantinople? He stood still in stunned silence as his wife approached him.

"Husband? Isn't all of this wonderful? I wondered how I could ever leave the house in Rome and its society, and it is all here now!"

The senator looked around him and there were some of the other villas that had neighbored theirs in Rome. He could not believe that Constantine had done it!

Constantine ensured that Constantinople grew at an alarming rate by adding incentives for the best and brightest to join him. For over 1000 years, this city became the center of learning, Christian thought, government, trade, art and industry. It was indeed a great legacy.

Just before Constantine died in 337, he asked to be baptised. He believed that baptism was important at the end of his life to ensure forgiveness for all of his sins. He died believing that he had received God's mercy and forgiveness and that he had done all he could to further God's name.

Cast of Characters

CONSTANTINE	Greek name for Flavius Valerius Constantinus
CONSTANTIUS CHLORUS	Constantine's father and Augustus of the West
CRISPUS	Constantine's first son by an earlier marriage
DIOCLETIAN	Emperor who divided power into four rulerships
FAUSTA	Constantine's scheming second wife
GALERIUS	Originally a Caesar emperor under Diocletian, later an Augustus

HELENA	Constantine's mother, later proclaimed a saint
LICINIUS	Augustus of the East at one time, co-signed the Edict of Milan
MAXIMIAN	One time Augustus of the West, father of Fausta and Maxientius
MAXENTIUS	Challenged Constantine for the position of Augustus of the West

About the Author:

Jocelyn James lives in Canberra, Australia with her husband and 4 boys. Before children, Jocelyn taught English, History, and Art at High School level and now, she is teaching her own children at home - with all its challenges and joys. Her favorite past times are reading, collecting books, drawing, writing and trying to find time to make cards. Jocelyn is active within the Australian homeschooling community - a contributor to the homeschooling magazine, *A Living Education* and Janette's Pictures of Australian History. Please check out her blog: www.homeschoolblogger.com/JocelynJames

Illustrations:

About the Illustrator:

 Darla Dixon is a self-taught portrait artist and illustrator who works primarily in graphite pencil (black and white) and colored pencil. Darla also illustrated an earlier book in this series *What Really Happened During the Middle Ages* also published by Bramley Books. Darla maintains a busy schedule with her home-based art business, creating fine art pencil portraits based on her client's provided photographs. When she isn't drawing, Darla enjoys scrapbooking, reading, and writing in her blog. Darla and her husband Mark live in the Atlanta, Georgia area and have four children.

You can find out more about Darla and her artwork by visiting her website at www.darladixon.com or by calling 770-736-1584.